**Proceedings of the 20th Annual
International Conference of the
Society for Phenomenology and Media**

SOCIETY FOR PHENOMENOLOGY AND MEDIA

proceedings

Publication of
The Society for Phenomenology and Media
Vol. 6, 2019

SOCIETY FOR PHENOMENOLOGY AND MEDIA

The Society for Phenomenology and Media

SPM Proceedings is the annual publication of the Society for Phenomenology and Media.

Copyrights for all essays are retained by their authors. Permission for republication can be obtained at glimpseSPM@gmail.com.

Republication must include a note citing this issue of SPM Proceedings as the place of original publication.

Copyright © 2019
All rights reserved.
ISBN-13: 978-1-7340540-1-9

SPM Officers (2018 – 2019)
President: Lars Lundsten
Vice President: Cristina Pontes Bonfiglioli
Secretary: Elvira Godek-Kiryluk

Treasurer: Luis Acebal

SPM Board of Directors (2018 – 2019)
Luis Acebal, National University, Redding, California, USA
Cristina Pontes Bonfiglioli, Centro Interdisciplinar de Semiótica da Cultura e da Mídia, Pontifical
    Catholic University of São Paulo, São Paulo, Brazil
Melinda Campbell, National University, La Jolla, California, USA
Alberto José Luis Carrillo Canán (Chair), Benemérita Universidad Autónoma de Puebla, Mexico
Gerardo de la Fuente, Universidad Nacional Autónoma de Mexico, Mexico City, Mexico
Alejandra de las Mercedes Fernández, Universidad Nacional del Nordeste, Resistencia, Argentina
Elvira Godek-Kiryluk, University of Illinois at Chicago, Chicago, USA
Jacques Ibanez Bueno, Université Savoie Mont Blanc, Chambéry, France
Stacey O'Neal Irwin, Millersville University of Pennsylvania, Millersville, Pennsylvania, USA
Matti Itkonen, University of Jyväskylä, Jyväskylä, Finland
Pieter Lemmens, Radboud University Nijmegen, Nijmegen, Netherlands
Nicola Liberati (Vice Chair), University of Twente, Enschede, Netherlands
Lars Lundsten, University of Akureyri, Akureyri, Iceland
Paul Majkut, National University, La Jolla, California, USA
Nyasha Mboti, University of Johannesburg, Johannesburg, South Africa
Shoji Nagataki, Chukyo University, Nagoya, Japan
José David Romero Martin, University of the Basque Country, Bilbao, Spain
Randall Dana Ulveland, Western Oregon University, Monmouth, Oregon, USA
Yoni Van Den Eede, Free University of Brussels, Brussels, Belgium
Tõnu Viik, Tallinn University, Tallinn, Estonia

SPM Advisory (2018 – 2019)
Mónica E. Alarcón Dávila, Universidad de Antioquia, Medellín, Columbia
Bas de Boer, University of Twente, Enschede, Netherlands
Adriana Durán Guerrero, Benemérita Universidad Autónoma de Puebla, Escuela de Artes
    Plásticas y Audiovisuales, Puebla, Mexico
Luanne Frank, University of Texas at Arlington, Arlington, Texas, USA
Miguel A. García, Hochschule Furtwangen, Furtwangen im Schwarzwald, Germany
Sophia Siddique Harvey, Vassar College, Poughkeepsie, New York, USA
Hye Young Kim, Husserl Archive, Ecole Normale Supérieure, Paris, France
Olga Kudina, University of Twente, Enschede, Netherlands
Sarah Lwahas, University of Jos, Plateau State, Jos, Nigeria
Lisa Neville, State University of New York, Cortland, USA
Obiageli Pauline Ohiagu, University of Port Harcourt, Nigeria
Melentie Pandilovski, Riddoch Art Gallery, Mount Gambier, Australia
Tracy Powell, Western Oregon University, Monmouth, Oregon, USA
Marleni Reyes Monreal, Benemérita Universidad Autónoma de Puebla, Escuela de Artes Plásticas
    y Audiovisuales, Puebla, Mexico
Dennis Skocz, Independent Scholar, Washington D. C., USA
James Steinhoff, University of Western Ontario, London, Ontario, Canada
T.J. Thomson, FHEA, Queensland University of Technology, Brisbane, Australia
Tales Tomaz, University of Salzburg, Salzburg, Austria
Marta Graciela Trógolo, Universidad Nacional del Nordeste, Resistencia, Chaco, Argentina
May Zindel, Unarte University, Puebla, Mexico

SPM *Proceedings* Editors: Elvira Godek-Kiryluk, *Managing Editor*
Melinda Campbell, *Assistant Editor*

SOCIETY FOR PHENOMENOLOGY AND MEDIA

PROCEEDINGS

UNIVERSITY OF AKUREYRI, AKUREYRI, ICELAND

SOCIETY FOR PHENOMENOLOGY AND MEDIA

Contents

INTRODUCTION PAUL MAJKUT	11
NEUROSCIENCE LITERACY AND THE SUGGESTIVENESS OF NEUROSCIENTIFIC EXPLANATIONS: BRAIN IMAGING TECHNOLOGIES AND THE CONSTITUTION OF NEUROSCIENTIFIC CONCEPTS BAS DE BOER	15
DOCUMENTARY FILM AND THE VISUAL CONSTRUCTION OF POVERTY ADRIANA DURÁN GUERRERO	25

THE DOUBLE SCREEN AND THE DEHISCENSE OF CORPOREALITY: A NEW FORM OF LITERACY
    ALEJANDRA DE LAS MERCEDES FERNÁNDEZ
    MARTA GRACIELA TRÓGOLO
    ROSARIO ZAPPONI
	33

HEIDEGGER'S DIGITS LUANNE FRANK	41
WEB 3.0 AND THE WEB OF LIFE. ATTUNING THE NOOSPHERE WITH (THE INTELLIGENCES OF) THE BIOSPHERE IN THE CONTEXT OF THE ANTHROPOCENE PIETER LEMMENS	49

NATIONAL IDENTITY, DOCUMENTATION, AND THE DIALOGICAL SELF TRACY POWELL	63
SURVEILLANCE THROUGH GAZE: MORALISTIC SELF-PRESENTATION AND MEDIATED BEHAVIOR TRACY POWELL	71
SURREALISM AS A WAY OF SEEING: ZYGMUNT BAUMAN ON ARTS IN LIQUID TIMES MARC VAN DEN BOSSCHE	77
THE ALGO-ARTIST GALIT WELLNER	87
CONTRIBUTORS	97

Introduction

The Twentieth International Conference of the Society for Phenomenology and Media took place at the University of Akureyri (*Háskólinn á Akureyri*) in Akureyri, Iceland.

Akureyri, a small city in the north of the country located on a beautiful Fjord, is graced by spectacular landscape and stunning *Aurora borealis,* and it is these Northern Lights that may serve as the motif of the conference: night light that illuminates the dark with unusual brilliance.

Though the climate was exceptionally cold to those who attended the conference, the university greeted participants with warmth and hospitality. Our host, Professor Lars Lundsten, brought together a diverse group of speakers from around the world as well as affording the opportunity for the free expression of widespread philosophical approaches. The theme of the conference, "'Global Media Literacy in the Digital Age," drew a variety of approaches to the topic, often sharply contrasting, always collegial. If a division of thought was apparent, it may be summarized as a difference between traditional epistemological and contemporary socio-economic approaches. This dialectic provided the conference with lively exchanges during ample panel follow-up discussion.

The essays included in *The Proceedings of the Twentieth International Conference of the Society for Phenomenology and Media* are arranged in alphabetical order.

In a sense, the tone of the conference was set by the keynote speaker, Professor Nyasha Mboti, of the Department of Communication Studies at the University of Johannesburg, South Africa. His current research, framing the emergence of a new theoretical paradigm for Apartheid Studies, set the intellectual parameters for all that followed.

Prof. Mboti's keynote, "Circuits of Apartheid: A Plea for Apartheid Studies," is available in the current edition of *Glimpse* (2019). n reading it, you will note a highly systematic style of thought that, again and again, "returns to the things themselves" in a manner not unfamiliar to phenomenologists. His use of historical data serves as a ground for his overall theory. Close observation of details brings his thought back to that ground. Often, he disabuses his audience of preconceived and uncritical assumptions. For example, in countering the reactionary attitude towards the poor that suggests that they need to understand the importance of a planned budget, he removes the ideological blindfold that often keeps philosophers from seeing "things in themselves," replying that the have-nots of the world do not need lectures from the haves on family budgeting. The poor are expert at budgeting, a necessity for daily survival. Indeed, it is the rich who need lessons on justice and a "balanced budget."

In the following pages, the division between socio-econo-political thought and epistemological attitudes towards global media literacy can be seen in two groups of essays. It should be pointed out, however, that the tradition in SPM is that participants are free to write on *any* aspect of media. SPM conference participants are free to ignore conference themes—as long as their papers are concerned with media in a broad sense.

If, for convenience, we may divide the papers in this volume into two groups, we find the following in what we may call the "epistemological group":

- Bas de Boer: "Neuroscience Literacy and the Suggestiveness of Neuroscientific Explanations: Brain Imaging Technologies and the Constitution of Neuroscientific Concepts."
- Alejandra de las Mercedes Fernández, Marta Graciela Trógolo, Rosario Zapponi: "The Double Screen and the Dehiscense of Corporeality: A New Form of Literacy."
- Luanne Frank: "Heidegger's Digits."
- Marc Van den Bossche: "Surrealism as a Way of Seeing: Zygmunt Bauman on Arts in Liquid Times."
- Galit Wellner: "The Algo-Artist."

The other grouping, the socio-econo-political, contains the remaining essays:

- Pieter Lemmens: "Web 3.0 and the Web of Life. Attuning the Noosphere with (the Intelligences of) the Biosphere in the Context of the Anthropocene."
- Tracy Powell: "National Identity, Documentation, and the Dialogical Self."
- Tracy Powell: "Surveillance through Gaze: Moralistic Self-Presentation and Mediated Behavior."

The counter-positioning of fundamental differences on how media should be approached not only made for a lively conference but widened the intellectual grasp of the Society.

SPM has always been a unique combination of philosophers and media theorists. What philosophers could not explain in terms of concrete practice, media theorists made clear. When media theorists neglected placing their theories in a larger context, philosophers took up the challenge.

The conference at the University of Akureyri was a test of the resiliency of SPM. The Twentieth International Conference of the Society for Phenomenology and Media in 2018 was planned for Winnipeg, Canada, but unforeseen problems meant a last-minute change. Prof. Lars Lundsten, an original founding member of SPM, stepped into the void and volunteered to host the conference. The policy of SPM is that our conferences rotate: Europe, North America, and Latin America. 2018 was set for the North American conference and, since Iceland is neither a part of Europe nor North America, it was a happy coincidence for which the Society is deeply indebted to Professor Lundsten and the University of Akureyri.

—Paul Majkut

Presentations in Alphabetical Order

Neuroscience Literacy and the Suggestiveness of Neuroscientific Explanations: Brain Imaging Technologies and the Constitution of Neuroscientific Concepts

BAS DE BOER

UNIVERSITY OF TWENTE
ENSCHEDE, THE NETHERLANDS

ABSTRACT: *In this paper, I will discuss the validity of the assumption that the simple presence of brain scans leads to an uncritical acceptance of neuroscientific explanations of human behavior and the extent to which developing a critical stance towards brain scans is necessary to create neuroscience literacy among citizens. Inspired by postphenomenology and the epistemology of Gaston Bachelard, I explore what a neuroscience literacy might encompass. As will become clear, this requires not only a critical stance towards brain scans per se but extends generally to the concepts used in the neurosciences and their relation to everyday life.*

First, I give an overview of sociological and social psychological studies addressing how an uncritical stance towards neuroscientific explanations among the lay public comes into being and how brain scans function within this process. Second, I will give a postphenomenological explanation for the potential suggestiveness of brain scans. Third, I turn to the epistemology of Gaston Bachelard in order to analyze how brain imaging technologies shape—and change—neuroscientific concepts and their relation to the lifeworld. Fourth, I show how understanding the processes through which neuroscientific concepts are constituted creates a starting point for understanding how neuroscientific explanations can be interpreted in a coherent (i.e., literate) manner. To conclude with, I suggest that neuroscience literacy leads us to a critical awareness of the hermeneutic processes through which the unproblematic transfer from the concepts within neuroscientific practices to the domain of everyday life is made.

KEYWORDS: neuroscience literacy, postphenomenology, Gaston Bachelard, brain imaging technologies, neurohype, philosophy of technology

INTRODUCTION

Neuroscientific explanations of human behavior have become increasingly influential due to technological developments that allow for the visualization of brain activity *in vivo*, most notably through the use of *functional Magnetic Resonance Imaging* (f(MRI)). In the last decades, large-scale projects in the neurosciences have received large amounts of public funding.[1] These projects bear the

---

[1] Neuroscientific research is far from a homogeneous category and consists of a wide variety of different practices and research topics (Pickersgill and Van Keulen xviii). For reasons of simplicity I decided to use the umbrella term "the neurosciences" to refer to the variety of explanatory purposes and practices within neuroscientific research.

promise to unravel the mysteries of the human mind accompanied with the idea that this would even potentially allow to intervene in the brain and change undesired patterns of behavior. This popularity is reflected in the increased media coverage of neuroscientific research—both in printed newspapers and online. Often, textual media coverage of neuroscientific discoveries displays brain scans, which is indicative of the importance of brain imaging technologies for the increased popularity of the neurosciences. It has been argued that these developments gave rise to a "neuro-hype" that leads to an uncritical acceptance of neuroscientific claims among the lay public (Ali et al. 1).[2] This prompts the question how to generate a public that is literate about neuroscientific research and capable of critically engaging with the outcomes of neuroscientific research (Baker et al. 256).

In this paper, I will discuss the validity of the assumption that the simple presence of brain scans leads to an uncritical acceptance of neuroscientific explanations of human behavior and the extent to which developing a critical stance towards brain scans is necessary to create neuroscience literacy among citizens. Inspired by postphenomenology and the epistemology of Gaston Bachelard, I explore what a neuroscience literacy might encompass. As will become clear, this requires not only a critical stance towards brain scans per se but extends generally to the concepts used in the neurosciences and their relation to everyday life.

First, I give an overview of sociological and social psychological studies addressing how an uncritical stance towards neuroscientific explanations among the lay public comes into being and how brain scans function within this process. Second, I will give a postphenomenological explanation for the potential suggestiveness of brain scans. Third, I turn to the epistemology of Gaston Bachelard in order to analyze how brain imaging technologies shape—and change—neuroscientific concepts and their relation to the lifeworld. Fourth, I show how understanding the processes through which neuroscientific concepts are constituted creates a starting point for understanding how neuroscientific explanations can be interpreted in a coherent (i.e., literate) manner. To conclude with, I suggest that neuroscience literacy leads us to a critical awareness of the hermeneutic processes through which the unproblematic transfer from the concepts within neuroscientific practices to the domain of everyday life is made.

BRAIN SCANS AND NEUROSCIENCE LITERACY

We live in a time in which

---

[2] For reasons of simplicity, I will use the term "lay public" to refer to citizens who are confronted with the media coverage of neuroscientific findings, while not involved in neuroscientific research themselves. This does not imply that I subscribe to the idea that there exists some kind of homogeneous "lay public" that appropriates media coverage of neuroscientific findings in a homogeneous manner. Neither should the use of "lay public" be considered as uncritically embracing the idea that there is a fundamental divide between neuroscientific experts and lay citizens. See also note 1.

neuroscientific explanations have a prominent place in the science sections of newspapers. Ali, Lifshitz, and Raz suggest that the increased media coverage of neuroscientific research and the seductive allure of neuroscientific explanations constitutes a *neuroenchantment* among the lay public (1). This enchantment might be further triggered by the fact that neuroscientists often use media articles to compete within their organizational environment and might benefit from positive and/or enchanting media coverage (Allgaier et al. 427). This does not imply, of course, that we should consider neuroscientists as blunt opportunists, but rather that creating a public capable of critically engaging with neuroscientific research might not be their primary interest. How do we then explain the source of this enchantment and how do we create a critical lay public that is capable of constructively engaging with neuroscientific claims?

"Neuroscientists have used brain scans to spot the difference between people who committed crimes on purpose and those who broke the law through sheer reckless behavior," starts Ian Sample's article entitled "Brain Scans Can Spot Criminal, Scientists Say" that appeared in *The Guardian* on March 2017.[3] As is typical of media coverage of neuroscience, this article is heavily accompanied with visualizations of the human brain obtained by (f)MRI. This creates an image of neuroscientific claims about human psychology as grounded in observable facts obtained by a rigorously *exact science*, rather than in philosophical *speculations* about the human psyche, thereby increasing the appearance of their trustworthiness. Researchers have been worried that this image of neurosciences creates a public that has unrealistic expectations about neuroscientific research and is incapable of developing a critical stance towards neuroscientific explanations (Dumit 8; Choudhury and Slaby 2). This problem gave rise to several sociological studies on the extent to which the presence of brain scans increases the likelihood that neuroscientific claims are believed by the lay public, regardless of the quality of argumentation.

The most recent review of empirical studies on this topic argues that research started by hypothesizing the existence of neuroimage bias or the idea that neuro*images* "may be overly influential to laypersons" (Baker et al. 252). For example, Racine, Bar-Ilan, and Illes found that the majority of media articles covering the neurosciences were uncritical of (f)MRI scans, likely generating a similar response among the public (136). This idea was confirmed in a study by McCabe and Castel that showed that brain images influence the perceived credibility of research in the cognitive neurosciences (349). However, this neuroimage bias was not replicated in all studies. For example, Hook and Farah found— much to their surprise—empirical evidence that brain images themselves had little influence on lay evaluations of neuroscience evidence, but that

---

[3] This paper is explicitly not concerned with assessing whether the neuroscientific claims that are covered in the media are actually true or reflect a consensus among the relevant community of neuroscientists but restricts itself to the seductive allure of neuroscientific explanations among the lay public.

invoking a neuroscientific vocabulary "enhance[s] the credibility of poorly reasoned arguments" used to explain human behavior (144). Furthermore, Schweitzer and Sacks showed that—based on an experiment that asked a jury to evaluate sources of legal evidence—the uncritical acceptance of neuroscientific claims can be explained in terms of the presence of a neuroscientific vocabulary (603). In their review, Baker, Ware, Schweitzer, and Risko argue that these contradicting results can be explained by taking into account that the persuasive power of brain scans is "very much dependent on context and framing" (252).

This brief summary indicates that the debate on why individuals are likely to accept neuroscientific explanations is far from settled: in some instances, it might be neuroimages that increase the credibility of neuroscientific explanations, while on other occasions this might be due to the presence of a neuroscientific vocabulary. However, empirical research *does* suggest that neuroscientific explanations have a certain seductive allure and that the capability of the lay public to critically engage with those explanations involves both *perceptual* and *conceptual* aspects. Accordingly, neuroscience literacy involves both a critical phenomenology of brain images and an understanding of the objects and concepts to which brain scans refer.

POSTPHENOMENOLOGY AND THE MULTISTABLE NATURE OF BRAIN SCANS

In the mid-2000s, when the popularity of (f)MRI was at its peak, Roskies warned that people intuitively equate neuroimages with photographs of the brain, but that there are important epistemological differences between the two (862). For example, the colors present in neuroimages present a statistically significant amount of activity in a certain brain area relative to the activity in the brain as a whole. Furthermore, (f)MRI does not measure brain activity directly, but measures the so-called BOLD-signal, which detects "changes in the ratio of oxygenated to deoxygenated blood that results from changes in blood flow and oxygen extraction" (Roskies 864). Thus, rather than being photograph-like depictions of the brain at a certain point in time, neuroimages are technical constructions that allow to draw inferences about the relation between brain activity and human behavior. Because of the intuitive appeal of neuroimages, these epistemological differences are often surpassed, thereby likely generating an inadequate understanding of their evidential status.

This dissimilarity with photographs does not imply that neuroimages are without epistemological value. Within the practices of neuroscientists, measures and visualizations of brain activity allow for discovering patterns of brain activity that correlate with different aspects of human behavior and cognition. For example, the possibility to visualize brain activity *in vivo* allows researchers to better understand the workings of clinical-pharmacological treatments by observing how they lead to an increase or decrease of activity in a certain brain area. The phenomenological appeal of brain scans thus also has a clear scientific merit when their specific epistemological qualities are taken into account. However, being able to critically engage with brain scans requires to interpret them in terms of the background in which they are generated.

The postphenomenological philosopher of technology Don Ihde has conceptualized the new ways in which technological developments open up new directions of scientific research and allow for new interpretations of reality in terms of the *technological mediation of scientific knowledge* (*Postphenomenology and Technoscience* 51). Departing from a phenomenological perspective, Ihde argues that technologies mediate relations between human beings and the world, thereby structuring how human beings are intentionally directed towards reality. Technologies actively help to shape human perceptions, actions, and interpretations. In the context of scientific practice, this implies that "increasingly many scientific phenomena are *technologically carpented* phenomena" (Ihde, *Instrumental Realism* 137). The objects of modern science are thus characterized as at least partly constituted by the technologies through which they are disclosed. This indicates that the reality investigated in scientific practices is partly constituted by the technologically mediated perceptions and interpretations of observed phenomena.

Ihde explicitly takes images generated by (f)MRI in the neurosciences as an example. He argues that (f)MRI translates previously invisible phenomena into images that are readable for embodied human beings. One of the characteristics of such images is what Ihde calls their *multistability*. Making an analogy with a Necker Cube, he argues that scientific images are gestalt-like images that allow for multiple coherent interpretations (*Experimental Phenomenology: Multistabilities* 146). This multistability indicates that science is a fundamentally *hermeneutic* affair: there is no such thing as nature that speaks to scientists in a direct manner, but neuroscientists are rather confronted with images that have to be actively read and interpreted, and that potentially give rise to a variety of coherent interpretations.

Considering scientific images in terms of multistability could explain why brain scans might have persuasive power: both for professional neuroscientists and lay people, brain images appear as an immediate gestalt and are accordingly treated as establishing an immediate link between the human brain and human behavior. However, the underlying hermeneutic processes are different: the strategies that scientists use to interpret brain scans might not necessarily overlap with the strategies of lay-people. As we will see, further investigating these different hermeneutic processes shows that these strategies have a different conceptual grounding.

BACHELARD'S PHENOMENO-TECHNIQUE: BRAIN IMAGING TECHNOLOGIES AND THE CONSTITUTION OF NEURO-SCIENTIFIC CONCEPTS

Although the concept of *multistability* points to the possibility for a brain scan to be interpreted in multiple coherent ways, it does not specifically address what is constitutive of a coherent interpretation. To address this latter issue, I turn to the epistemology of a French philosopher of science, Gaston Bachelard.

Bachelard argues that the objects in the sciences do not exist in nature but are *artificially* realized within scientific practices. In a Bachelardian sense, the term "artificial" is not used to disqualify scientific research. On the contrary, it is precisely through the artificiality of scientific objects that their rational (i.e., scientific) character is constituted. For example, he argues that science "must be formed against nature, against all that comes from nature's impetus and instruction, within us and outside us, against natural allurements and colourful, diverse facts" (*The Formation of the Scientific Mind* 33). Consequently, the specific concepts that are used to describe scientific objects are contingent on the way these objects are realized. Bachelard uses the term *phenomenotechnique* to conceptualize the processes within which scientific objects come into being: "Science *realizes* its objects without ever just finding them ready-made. Phenomenotechnique *extends* phenomenology. A concept becomes scientific in so far as it becomes a technique, in so far as it is accompanied by a technique that realizes" (*The Formation of the Scientific Mind* 70). This indicates that the constitution of scientific objects is not simply a matter of the perceptual observation of new phenomena but should be understood in terms of how these phenomena appear within a constellation of available technologies, existing scientific theories and concepts, and the experimental setup in which they appear.

Bachelard's term "technique" in "phenomenotechnique" should not be unproblematically identified with the technical manner in which scientific phenomena become visible. As he points out, a scientist should not be understood as a *Homo Faber*, but rather as being concerned with "amplify[ing] what is revealed beyond appearance" (*The Formation of the Scientific Mind* 13). Bachelard paradigmatic examples to explain this idea are taken from physics: scientific objects such as electrodes do not exist independent of a phenomenotechnique, so making a judgment that an observed phenomenon can be understood as an electron requires not only perception, but also relating a perceived phenomenon to the concepts used in theories within physics (*The New Scientific Spirit* 6). This explains why Bachelard holds that phenomenotechnique *extends* phenomenology: it is the revealing of what is beyond appearance through the use of scientific concepts that allow us to make sense of the perceived phenomenon.

Recently, Borck has argued that "the brain must be understood as an artifact in the precise sense of the Bachelard had in mind when he described modern physics" (119), indicating that the brain as a research object is subject to continuous change because of the different ways it is realized within a phenomenotechnique.[4] In addition, I would add that this idea can be extended to the objects of the

---

[4] Bachelard specifically developed his ideas on the constitution of scientific objects within in a phenomenotechnique in the context of physics. A critical discussion of the exact limits of Bachelard's phenomenotechnique is beyond the scope of this paper. For present purposes, I uncritically assume that Bachelard's notion of phenomenotechnique can be applied outside the restricted domain of physics.

cognitive neurosciences, e.g., aggression, emotions, visual attention, which are specifically constituted in their relation with the way they can be linked to brain activity because of the presence of brain imaging technologies. Adopting this perspective allows to understand the coherency of possible interpretations of brain scans in terms of their relation to the specific way in which the objects of the neurosciences are constituted in neuroscientific practice. If the constitution of the objects of the neurosciences is indeed dependent on the particular phenomenotechnique within neuroscientific practices, the relevant question in the context of developing neuroscience literacy is thus whether or not the specific phenomenotechnique in which neuroscientific concepts are developed can be unproblematically extended to the domain of everyday life.

WHAT CONSTITUTES A COHERENT INTERPRETATION OF NEUROSCIENTIFIC CLAIMS?

Asking to what extent the concepts of the neurosciences can be transferred to the domain of everyday life brings us back to the question what constitutes a coherent interpretation of neuroimages. If the cognitive-psychological concepts that neuroscientists use do not refer to the same cognitive-psychological phenomena we speak about in everyday life, a coherent interpretation of a neuroimage should take this difference into account.

Francken and Slors have discussed this problematic in terms of the "translational problem" of the neurosciences. They argue that although the concepts of the neurosciences are often derived from what they call the common-sense concepts that we use to explain human behavior, these common-sense concepts need to be refined and operationalized in order to be experimentally linked to brain activity. This process "involves multiple interpretational steps" that significantly change the meaning of the initial common-sense concept ("Neuroscience and Everyday Life" 68).[5] For example, the neuroscience of love is usually studied in terms of "a passive, emotional experience in response to seeing a picture of a beloved. Although there might be good scientific reasons to studying love in this manner, these nuances are lost when neuroscientific claims about love are translated to everyday life. Hence, they argue that neuroscientific concepts cannot be unproblematically applied in the domain of everyday life.

A second aspect of the translation problem is that the vocabulary of the neurosciences has a different style of explanation, than the explanations we use to explain human behavior in everyday life. For example,

---

[5] Among the different neurosciences, a similar "translational problem" seems to be present because there is not a singular way in which common sense concepts are refined and operationalized ("From Commonsense to Science, and Back" 249). Although Francken and Slors make no reference to the philosophy of Bachelard and the idea that scientific objects are constituted within a specific phenomenotechnique, their call for developing a shared cognitive *ontology* among the different neurosciences suggests that the coming into being of scientific objects can be considered an ontological event that can be understood in Bachelardian terms.

neuroscientists might point to increased activity in the *left insula* as causing an individual's inability to pay attention to his or her environment. However, in everyday life, explanations of behavior often have an additional function, because they also are used to "justify and excuse actions and make them 'understandable'" ("Neuroscience and Everyday Life" 70). In this context, reference to 'activity in the left insula' might be used to justify why someone is not paying attention to his conversational partner and also suggest that he can be excused for this. The purposes for which a neuroscientific vocabulary is applied in this latter case is significantly different from the purposes of the strict laboratory setting in which the vocabulary was developed.

Pointing out these two aspects of the translational problem of neuroscience does not imply that we should principally refrain from integrating the neuroscientific vocabulary in our everyday lives— even if it *would* be practically possible to do so. However, addressing these two aspects might help explain what constitutes a coherent interpretation of neuroscientific findings, and what it would mean for a lay public to display some form of neuroscience literacy. Conceptualizing neuroscience literacy in these terms has the additional advantage that adopting a critical stance towards neuroscientific findings does not necessarily mean to engage in the painstaking process of getting acquainted with the technical vocabulary of the neurosciences. Rather, it forces us to reflect on what we mean when we use psychological concepts in everyday life and to what extent invoking a neuroscientific vocabulary is in accordance with this use. In line with Georges Canguilhem's advice in the context of the history of science, an important aspect of neuroscience literacy is to refrain from "thinking that persistent use of a particular term indicates an invariant underlying concept" (32).

CONCLUSION: TOWARDS A CRITICAL NEUROENCHANTMENT

As I hope to have made clear, when discussions about neuroscience literacy focus on the seductive allure of neuroscientific explanations, either in terms of neuroimages or in terms of a specific neuroscientific vocabulary, they neglect the deeper hermeneutic problem in which the unproblematic transfer from the concepts within neuroscientific practices to the domain of everyday life is made. In this paper, I have suggested that this deeper hermeneutic problem can be addressed when distinguishing on the one hand between the phenomenotechnique in which the objects of the neurosciences are constituted and brain scans attain a particular meaning and, on the other, the everyday life circumstances in which we use psychological concepts to explain and justify the behavior of ourselves and of others.

To conclude with, I want to stress that my analysis is not principally at odds with some form of neuroenchantment. The question this paper dealt with is how neuroscience literacy can be understood as being *critically* enchanted by coming to a coherent interpretation of neuroscientific claims. Comparing the hermeneutic processes within which the objects of the neurosciences are constituted and through which neuroscientists interpret brain scans and use them to make neuroscientific claims *vis-à-vis* the hermeneutic processes through which we interpret neuroscientific claims in everyday life might help developing such a critical neuroenchantment.

WORKS CITED

Ali, Sabrina, S., Michael Lifshitz, and Amir Raz. "Empirical Neuroenchantment: From Reading Minds to Thinking Critically." *Frontiers in Human Neuroscience*, vol. 8, article 357, 2014, pp. 1-4.

Allgaier, Joachim, Sharon Dunwoody, Dominique Brossard, Yin-Yueh Lo, and Hans Peter Peters. "Medialized Science? Neuroscientist's Reflections on their Role as Journalistic Sources." *Journalism Practice*, vol. 7, no. 4, 2013, pp. 413-429.

Bachelard, Gaston. *The New Scientific Spirit*. Translated by Arthur Goldhammer, Beacon Press, 1984.

Bachelard, Gaston. *The Formation of the Scientific Mind: A Contribution to a Psychoanalysis of Objective Knowledge*. Translated by Mary McAllester-Jones, Clinamen Press, 2002.

Baker, D.A., Jillian M. Ware, N.J. Schweitzer, and Evan F. Risko. "Making Sense of Research on the Neuroimage Bias." *Public Understanding of Science*, vol. 26, no.2, 2017, pp. 251-258.

Borck, Cornelius. "How We May Think: Imaging and Writing Technologies across the History of the Neurosciences." *Studies in History and Philosophy of Science Part C: Studies in History and Philosophy of Biological and Biomedical Sciences*, vol. 57, 2016, pp. 112-120.

Canguilhem, Georges. *Etudes d'Histoire et de Philosophie des Sciences Concernant les Vivant et la Vie*. Vrin, 1994.

Choudhury, Suparna, and Jan Slaby, editors. *Critical Neuroscience: A Handbook of the Social and Cultural Contexts of Neuroscience*. Wiley-Blackwell, 2012.

Dumit, Joseph. *Picturing Personhood: Brain Scans and Biomedical Identity*. Princeton University Press, 2004.

Francken, Jolien C., and Marc Slors. "From Commonsense to Science, and Back: The Use of Cognitive Concepts in Neuroscience." *Consciousness and Cognition*, vol. 29, 2014, pp. 248-258.

Francken, Jolien C., and Marc Slors. "Neuroscience and Everyday Life: Facing the Translation Problem." *Brain and Cognition*, vol. 120, 2018, pp. 67-74.

Hook, Cayce J., and Martha J. Farah. "Look Again: Effect of Brain Images and Mind-Brain Dualism on Lay Evaluations of Research." *Journal of Cognitive Neuroscience*, vol. 25, no. 9, 2013, pp. 1397-1405.

Ihde, Don. *Instrumental Realism: The Interface between Philosophy of Science and Philosophy of Technology*. Indiana University Press, 1991.

Ihde, Don. *Postphenomenology and Technoscience: The Peking University Lectures*. Suny Press, 2009.

Ihde, Don. *Experimental Phenomenology: Multistabilities*. 2nd ed., Suny Press, 2012.

McCabe, David P., and Alan D. Castel. "Seeing Is Believing: The Effect of Brain Images on Judgments of Scientific Reasoning." *Cognition*, vol. 107, 2008, pp. 343-352.

Pickersgill, Martin, and Ira Van Keulen, editors. *Sociological Reflections on the Neurosciences*. Emerald Group Publishing, 2011.

Racine, Eric, Ofek Bar-Ilan, and Judy Illes. "Brain Imaging: A Decade of Coverage in the Print Media." *Science Communication*, vol. 28, no. 1. 2006, pp. 122-143.

Roskies, Adina L. "Are Neuroimages Like Photographs of the Brain?" *Philosophy of Science*, vol. 74, no. 5, 2007, pp. 860-872.

Sample, Ian. "Brain Scans Can Spot Criminals, Scientists Say." *The Guardian*, 17 Mar. 2017, www.theguardian.com/science/2017/mar/13/brain-scans-can-spot-criminals-scientists-say. Accessed 27 August 2018.

Schweitzer, N.J., and Michael J. Saks. "Neuroimage Evidence and the Insanity Defense." *Behavioral Science & the Law*, vol. 29, 2011, pp. 592-607.

Documentary Film and the Visual Construction of Poverty

ADRIANA DURÁN GUERRERO

BENEMÉRITA UNIVERSIDAD AUTÓNOMA DE PUEBLA
ESCUELA DE ARTES PLÁSTICAS Y AUDIOVISUALES
PUEBLA, MEXICO

ABSTRACT: *To understand the moving image as a tool of mediation is to take advantage of the use of a camera as a communicative instrument capable of influencing the way in which we represent the world. The visual construction of poverty, through the moving image in a documentary film, links the knowledge of a documentary film and visual studies. It is necessary to reflect on what happens in our minds when they are influenced by the multitude of images that we see in our daily life. Poverty, as a result of how we build it visually, must be understood as a complex social phenomenon and requires a Marxist critique of the visuality of the dominant class. In this context, visuality and countervisuality are both considered as terms in film studies. In the context of economic and political groups that rule the world, visuality and countervisuality are used to compare the visual constructions of power in a documentary film that helps us understand the face of poverty. In this article, the genre of documentary film is proposed as a possibility of a different visual construction.*

KEYWORDS: documentary, film, visuality, construction, representation

Understanding moving photography in terms of its mediation tool, that is through the use of a camera as a communicative instrument capable of influencing the form of representation of the world, allows the study of film in terms of image and visual construction, which determines a relationship with a theme (Arvéndol 2). This paper takes up a study of how documentary visually constructs poverty and argues for a possibility that what issues from visual construction is distinct from what emanates from power, which I define as the economic, political, or social control of a society, and from its use of images to maintain its authority over society. Beyond what can be seen as an economic problem, I identify poverty as a visual problem.

Knowing where the film is being seen brings forth a conversation that marks the context from which to identify the type of visual construction encountered and how much it has appropriated our structures and social connections. According to Carl Plantinga, documentary film is a constructed representation of reality, which means, it is a visual representation of the world in which we live bordering a perspective of the filmmaker (67). For cinematographers, the context is primordial in taking on themes audio-visually. Francesco Casetti, who proposes the importance of the context for the understanding of a phenomenon, in this case, a film, defends this premise:

The film associates itself with the social environment in which it finds itself, with its necessities, habits, expectations, and ways of doing things; at the moment and place in which it is produced and is projected; the action of who makes it and who enjoys it, with their respective orientations, intentions, and abilities; to the combination of texts that they accompany […] In one word, the text (film-related) takes place in the relationship with its context, or, with its surrounding in which it operates or at least attempts to operate. (Casetti 286)

On the other hand, we should not stop taking into consideration the recipient of audiovisual discourse, specifying that:

> the addressee of the cinematographic product is also situated in visually "reading" the reality that encircles a range of collective environments: he or she also expresses pure and simple optical presence of acts and customs. (Passolini 10)

Documentary film is about presenting society from within a common consensus: what we see on the screen forms part of our historic world, and this premise adds value to the verisimilitude of the public. When a documentary is projected, it can represent the voice of the filmmaker and whomever he puts onto the screen, which is to say, it audio-visually represents a vision of the world without forgetting the fact that the recorded is real, but does not completely answer the question about the scene setting as some objectivists would like to ensure (Niney 61). Additionally, the montage is inserted providing a narrative sense.

In Latin America, documentary film has had an aesthetic and discursive journey that can be explained from within the historic events that have happened. It has touched on themes such as poverty, which projects a treatment of the socio-economic and political situation of countries from diverse points of view and forms of filmmaking. However, documentary film has been characterized as being an under-recognized platform for dominant institutions in terms of commercial exhibition. In Mexico, for instance, documentary film is typically projected in alternative spaces, very few of which are considered commercial spaces, which prevents greater exposure to the public. In this sense, as time passed, fiction became more popular in terms of the exhibitor interest in the documentary and audience consumption of a greater quantity of fictitious films. As a product of such marginality, the documentary film fostered a space for experimentation and open manifestation of ideas permitting producers to touch themes of all kinds and develop their own aesthetic language (IMCINE 206).

For the full-length documentary, earning time on cinematographic screens has been a complex process in both political and economic realms. The Mexican Institute of Cinematography asserts in its "Annual Statistics of Mexican Film 2011" that the majority of documentary films have not captured the interest of exhibitors due to their low sales expectations or because some of their themes are not well-regarded by authorities (IMCINE 207). These kinds of situations, added to the low box-office expectations of documentaries, have provoked large contrasts even between fiction and non-fiction displays.

Poverty defames human integrity, deteriorates social fabric, and makes basic necessities impossible for those who suffer. According to Amartya Sen, poverty is the lack of ability to make one's own living, where one can see the inability to live a human life as one would see humanly fit (194-98). In Mexico, according to the government institution National Committee of Social Development Policy (CONEVAL), in 2010 there were 46.2% poor people, or around 52.8 million people in the country were living in poverty (1).[1] However, this year, Julio Boltvinik, a Mexican academic, pointed out in *La Jornada* that 80.7% of the Mexican population are poor. The difference between these percentages completely changes the conversation, from my perspective, because aside from marking a social problem, it marks a field of analysis from which one could ask, how is poverty "seen"?

The conversation on poverty represents different institutions including the publicity sector, politics, government, among others, equaling the dominant part of society—that of power. For example, the mediation of CONEVAL, maintained as an official speech source and medium, allied companies and publicity strategists, which played an important role in how this mediation encouraged behaviors related to shame and consumption.

According to Nicholas Mirzoeff visuality or "visuality complexes," that is, the historic explanations of society, contribute to organize society with an objective of legitimizing social structures that define how we see and explain the world (Martinez 25). In other words, visuality is the combination of images infused into our thinking thanks to images with dominant discourse from power. In relationship to the rate of poverty, the dominant discourse of "shame" is spread through bank automatic transaction machines by means of moving images and photographs asking for donations for poor children or in supermarkets by asking shoppers to round up amounts for those who do not have anything to eat, etc. One hero dynamic taken by Thomas Carlyle is that even our typical days relate directly with the vision of power (Dussel 73). Under this social dynamic, we feel like the heroes of others—of the poor ones. This gives the impression that poverty stops being a social and collective concern and transforms poverty into a spectacle of consumption and shame where the unfortunate will be saved by the more fortunate: poverty exists but you with your donation or help can contribute to eradicating it; the poor need you and thank you for it. In contrast to these and similar consumer experiences enabled by the spectacle of poverty, Mexican documentary films like *The Heirs* by Eugenio Polgovsky (2008) and *The*

---

[1] See works cited for a complete citation and link.

Forgotten Tree by Luis Rincón (2009) ground a profound vision of poverty and its root problems and give voice to diverse conversations about inheritance, poverty, and the impossibility of getting out of poverty. According to the synopsis of the film on the Ibermedia website, *The Heirs* constructs the vision of rural poverty through the representation of children, while the Morelia Film Festival website reminds us that *The Forgotten Tree* constructs the vision of urban poverty through the representation of relations between a girl, her mother, her aunt, and a young man.

Niney affirms that the best bet of documentary film is to interrogate the world, which in essence is subjective, looking to reveal visual angles and a meaningful montage (37). Documentary film has been associated with stories based on information and compared to narratives that present opposing information as in the aptly named "guerrilla filmic war" (Aviña 23-4). For example, *Aristegui Noticias*, an important news website in Mexico, reminds us of Canal 6 de Julio with the documentary film *Chronicle of a Fraud* (1988), which presents a narrative opposite to the government at that time. In this sense, the documentary can inform another perspective to contrast those images emitted from power. According to Carlos Mendoza Aupetit, a documentarist from Canal 6 de Julio, filmic war is produced when the active spectator gives life to the massive diffusion of certain documentaries that contradict official propaganda campaigns and that have given place to small media setbacks to the government and its allies (9).

The possibility of documentary film as a distinct visual construction to the dominant discourse will depend on the posture that the maker wants to take on in the theme that develops in commitment to the historic world that surrounds it, informing, investigating, observing, etc. For example, a 2010 documentary from director Luis Rincón, *The Forgotten Tree*, records excerpts from daily lives of people who fight to get out of the spiral of violence and poverty in which they live. It was recorded in the same place as was, fifty years ago, Luis Buñuel's *The Forgotten*. The documentary emphasizes that despite the passage of time this place remains in the same social conditions of poverty. Morelia Film Festival synopsis of the film shows us that decisions made by the characters submerge them time after time in urban misery without a possibility of escaping their tragic destiny. The primary discourse has to do with the marginalization of the poor in the urban sector of Mexico City. It's about hopelessness, constantly showing how the characters cannot get out of socially conditioned poverty for generations and there is no hope of ever doing it.

The filmmaker, Luis Rincón, went through various processes before delimiting the central theme of the documentary. Little by little, the influence of Buñuel's *The Forgotten* and the Nonoalco zone fifty years later acquired new elements that became principal objectives in the documentary:

> What I wanted to revisit was the condition of poverty in this zone and the only way I could do it, in principle, was revisiting it in a physical form, that is to

say, they live in cardboard boxes, houses have only one bed that everyone shares, etc. Soon one stigmatizes or because of prejudice one believes that people there are criminals and do nothing except commit crimes, or beg for money, and do drugs, etc. I got to know the people and I realized that the movie could not be only about poverty, I advanced in my investigation, and I realized that the movie could be about something else. I feel that the end of the movie is about the dreams of the characters, about what they hold on to and how poverty then seen as the physical conditions of one's home ended up becoming a labyrinth of dead ends where although you want to and desire to improve yourself and move forward the conditions around you will never permit that. (Rincón, Interview)

Luis Rincón dedicated hours every day to field investigation—meeting and getting to know people in order to enrich the point of view of the producer—and this added to the visual experience of the documentary's discourse. This premise, emphasizes the possibility of a distinct look at the visual hegemony constructed from power:

You never have hope, I ended up planting poverty in the film in this, the lack of hope of the characters to get out and get on with their lives. I believe that that is the most powerful kind of poverty and the movie visits and revisits that. At the end of the documentary the objective was: to make a film that talks about the tragedy of the people that have no way to get out and to move forward. (Rincón, Interview)

The method shows the context and how the people tend to interact in everyday life, which permits getting to know the visual constructions closely, as if the public were there, like a witness. On the other hand, the observational style breaks down at some critical moments in the movie, putting an emphasis on interviews done in a participative fashion, where the producer comes in contact with the social actors (Cock 67). The participative approach can be used to emphasize the perspective of the people that are taken in during the theme which in this case is poverty. These techniques seek to bring in the public with whomever you see on the screen, a close up with one another.

In the first minutes of *The Forgotten Tree*, we can hear a sound that contextualizes a Mexico where television talks about poverty from within soap operas and commercials and asks for aid for people in need. The representation of commercials juxtaposed with the representation of social actors in front of the camera at the same time provides us with two contrasting constructions of poverty. Commercials seem so close to the social actors because they are watching television, yet they remain far with respect to the message that they look to transmit. Witnessing the projection from the perspective of those who suffer poverty makes the public think about the paradox between what is told via the television and what is seen in the house on the other side. One distinct vision, countervisual.

In Inés Dussel's interview with Nicholas Mirzoeff, the theorist of contemporary visual culture defines countervisuality as "the possibility of the citizenship that can create a visual map of the social" (74). The visual map of the social involves a distinct vision of the social: it is a way to know a counterhistory of visuality, a decolonization of the look of a visuality that dictates and supervises the distribution of what can be said, seen, and looked at (Martínez 27). In this sense, documentary films like *The Forgotten Tree* or *The Heirs* can be part of countervisuality, constructing one of multiple visions of the social through creative treatment of the observed and adding aesthetic and artistic purpose to visual construction. The work of the filmmakers becomes important, given that in their practices they carry out media and communication related functions that can construct distinct visual realities of our environment. The producer, as a creator of discourse with images, balances in aesthetics the vitality and beauty of his work, emphasizes the discursive power of the image, and--by means of audiovisual language--adds a life experience (Mendoza 95).

With countervisuality, it would be valid to analyze a documentary one after another to destabilize the conversations that authority dictates on specific themes by navigating diverse postures that inform us in distinct ways. Understanding the power of image in our context is essential for the documentarist: it is still a great commitment for those who plan on speaking about our surroundings through the language of documentary film. Upon doing the audiovisual project, the filmmaker becomes a visual constructor of reality, which adds to the power of the consensus that the documentary theater already has, when the public assumes that what we are projecting on the screen is part of reality.

We can affirm that poverty constitutes a visual problem in addition to being an economic one. We define, represent, and talk about it from distinct perspectives. Visual construction of poverty can be different according to the social institution (or function) that emanates from it. The investigation around documentary film from my perspective is of great importance in multiples senses. I consider that the documentary film, among other things, is a communicative tool of great value. Recognizing it as an important communicative actor in our context can place it in a conscious state that can be seen and portrayed as much for the producer as for the public. Image, as one of the most important elements in cinematographic language, recognizes its own great discursive power, not only for the producer but also for the public and for political or economic institutions which govern our context. It is further worth noting that the study of image in documentary film leaves open a variety of possible themes that an investigator could examine in a detailed analysis of the democratic use of images and their visual construction.

WORKS CITED

"Annual Statistics of Mexican Film 2011." *Mexican Institute of Cinematography*. IMCINE, 2011, mptests.info/wp-content/uploads/CINEMEXICA

NO/ANUARIOESTADISTICO/Anuario_Estadistico_de_Cine_Mexicano_2011.pdf. Accessed 20 February 2018.

"Chapter IX: Statistical Recounting of 1910-2011." *Mexican Institute of Cinematography.* IMCINE, 2011, mptests.info/wp-content/uploads/CINEMEXICANO/ANUARIOESTADISTICO/Anuario_Estadistico_de_Cine_Mexicano_2011.pdf. Accessed 11 February 2018.

"CONEVAL informa los resultados de la medición de pobreza 2010: Comunicado de prensa no. 007" [CONEVAL Reports the Results of Poverty Measurement 2010: Press Release no. 007"]. *CONEVAL: Consejo Nacional de Evaluacion de la Politica de Desarrollo Social [National Council for the Evaluation of Social Development Policy].* 29 July 2011, docreader.readspeaker.com/docreader/?jsmode=1&cid=bzyxi&lang=es_mx&url=https%3A%2F%2Fwww.coneval.org.mx%2Finformes%2FPobreza%25202010%2FCOMUNICADO_PRENSA_MEDICION_DE_POBREZA_2010.pdf&autotag=0&v=Apple%20Computer,%20Inc. Accessed 10 June 2019.

"How Was Canal 6 de Julio Born?... And Its New Documentary about an Earthquake (#AnInterview)." *Aristegui Noticias,* 19 October 2017. m.aristeguinoticias.com/1910/mexico/como-nacio-el-canal-6-de-julio-y-su-nuevo-documental-sobre-el-sismo-laentrevista/. Accessed 10 June 2019.

"Los Herederos" ["The Heirs"]. *Programa Ibermedia: El Espacio Audiovisual Iberoamericano,* March 2013, www.programaibermedia.com/ibermediatv/los-herederos/. Accessed 10 June 2019.

"El árbol olvidado" ["The Forgotten Tree"]. *Festival Internacional del Cine en Morelia: Directorio de Películas [Morelia International Film Festival: Film Directory],* Tenth Morelia International Film Festival, 18-27 October 2019, moreliafilmfest.com/peliculas/el-arbol-olvidado/. Accessed 10 June 2019.

Arvéndol, Elisenda. "Through an Anthropology of the Glance: Ethnography, Representation, and Construction of Audiovisual Information." *Magazine of Dialectology and Popular Traditions,* vol LIII, no. 2, 1998, dra.revistas.csic.es/index.php/dra/article/viewFile/396/400. Accessed 5 February 2018.

Aviña, Rafael. *An Insolite Glance: Themes and Genres of Mexican Film.* Océano: Cineteca Nacional, 2004: 23-24.

Boltvinik, Julio. "Economía Moral [Moral Economy]." *La Jornada,* 13 April 2012, www.jornada.com.mx/2012/04/13/opinion/028o1eco. Accessed 21 October 2017.

Casetti, Francesco. *Theories of Film 1945-1990.* Madrid: Cátedra, 2010: 286.

Cock Peláez, Alejandro. *Analysis of the Rhetorical Elements of Non-Fiction Film in the Post Truth Era [Retóricas del Cine de No Ficción en La Era de La Post Verdad].* 2012. Autonomous University of Barcelona, Ph.D. Dissertation, ddd.uab.cat/pub/tesis/2011/hdl_10803_96533/acp1de1.pdf. Accessed 10 June 2019.

Dussell, Inés. "Entrevista con

Nicholas Mirzoeff. La cultura visual contemporánea: política y pedagogía para este tiempo" ["Interview with Nicholas Mirzoeff. Contemporary Visual Culture: Politics and Pedagogy for This Time."] *Propuesta Educativa*, no. 31, 2009, p. 69-79, Facultad Latinoamericana de Ciencias Sociales Buenos Aires, Argentina, www.redalyc.org/pdf/4030/40304 1703007.pdf. Accessed 10 June 2019.

Martinez Luna, Sergio. "Visuality in Question and the Right to Look." *Chilean Journal of Visual Anthropology [Revista Chilena de Antropología Visual]*, no. 19, June 2012, pp. 20-36, www.antropologiavisual.cl/martinez_luna.html#9. Accessed 10 June 2019.

Mendoza, Carlos. *Canal 6 de Julio: la guerrilla fílmica: comunicación alternativa documental y autogestión [Canal 6 de Julio: Guerrilla Film War: Alternative Documentary Communication and Self-Management]*. Heródoto, 2008, pp. 9-12.

Mendoza, Carlos. *The Script for Documentary Film*. University Center of Cinematographic Studies: UNAM, 2011.

Niney, François. *The Proof of What Is Real Is on the Screen*. University Center of Cinematographic Studies: UNAM, 2009.

Passolini, Pier Paolo. *Cinema: The Movie as Semiology of Reality*. University Center of Cinematographic Studies: UNAM, 2006.

Plantinga, Carl. *Retórica y representación en el cine de no ficción* [Rhetoric and representation of nonfiction cinema]. University Center of Cinematographic Studies: UNAM, 2014.

Rincón, Luis. Personal interview. 3 April 2014.

Sen, Amartya. "The Possibility of Social Choice." NobelPrize.org, Nobel Media AB 2019, www.nobelprize.org/prizes/economic-sciences/1998/sen/lecture/. Accessed 27 June 2019.

The "Double Screen" and the Dehiscense of Corporeality: A New Form of Literacy

ALEJANDRA DE LAS MERCEDES FERNÁNDEZ
MARTA GRACIELA TRÓGOLO
ROSARIO ZAPPONI

UNIVERSIDAD NACIONAL DEL NORDESTE
RESISTENCIA, ARGENTINA

ABSTRACT: *The double screen or second screen is an effect of ultra-mediatization since it naturalizes the fact of having access to the world of experience through devices outside the field of the senses. In the original sense, a screen is something that both shows and hides, which is to say that its existence as an artifact constitutes a kind of barrier. It lets us see to point out that it conceals something or interrupts a certain continuity of space. A screen always superimposes an order of being on another order of reality. Every device is a result of engineering away from the functionality of nature as a source of morphological principles for technology. What characterizes the "secondness" of a screen is its continued daily use.* [1]

There is a performative preeminence of devices—interpreted as screens—in any field, which is at the same time the condition of existence for all possible representations and executions. The question is whether this convergence between bodies as artificial devices and our own bodies in their capacity as "devices" suffices or whether the experiential forms of corporality are relegated to the mediate possibilities of profuse amplification under forms of images. Corporality as an immediate statement of existence is disproved by the polysemy executed by devices translated simply as "screens." The dehiscence of the bodies is the evidence of how the world of life, as conceived by Husserl, must now be re-signified through the experience of mediatization as a form of new literacy.

KEYWORDS: second screen, devices, central nervous system, dehiscence, new literacy

> "But the face of Big Brother seemed to persist for several seconds on the screen, as though the impact that it had made on everyone's eyeballs was too vivid to wear off immediately. The little sandy haired woman had flung herself forward over the back of the chair in front of her. With a tremulous murmur that sounded like 'My Saviour!' she extended her arms towards the screen. Then she buried her face in her hands. It was apparent that she was uttering a prayer."
> George Orwell, *1984* (Part1, Chapter 1)

---

[1] One of the newest experiences when visiting old buildings in France is to find oneself obliged to resort to screen devices as a condition of having a "real experience" of that visit.

INTRODUCTION:

The double screen or second screen is an effect of ultra-mediatization since it naturalizes the fact of having access to the world of experience through devices outside the field of the senses. In the original sense, a screen is something that both shows and hides, which is to say that its existence as an artifact constitutes a kind of barrier. It lets us see to point out that it conceals something or interrupts a certain continuity of space. A screen always superimposes an order of being on another order of reality. Every device is a result of engineering away from the functionality of nature as a source of morphological principles for technology. What characterizes the "secondness" of a screen is its continued daily use. [8]

There is a performative pre-eminence of devices—interpreted as screens—in any field, which is at the same time the condition of existence for all possible representations and executions. The question is whether this convergence between bodies as artificial devices and our own bodies in their capacity as "devices" suffices or whether the experiential forms of corporality are relegated to the mediate possibilities of profuse amplification under forms of images. Corporality as an immediate statement of existence is disproved by the polysemy executed by devices translated simply as "screens." The dehiscence of the bodies is the evidence of how the world of life, as conceived by Husserl, must now be re-signified through the experience of mediatization as a form of new literacy.

TOPICS
1. TERMINOLOGICAL AMBIGUITY. WHAT IS THE SCREEN?

Talking screen does not necessarily lead to the etymological origin of the term, and it is essential to clarify its material significance to the pragmatics of its uses as a word and as a thing. In Spanish language this origin is very interesting, since it seems to come from the old Catalan "*pampolla,*" derived from the Latin "*pampanus,*" a hanging set of vine branches, which was placed in the background to separate outdoor environments, and also of the word "*ventall,*" which means a crack in the wall for the wind to pass through. In its corrupted form the word "*Ventana,*" which means window, arises. In the English language, it is that which interposes, that which does not allow to pass or which filters as if it were a curtain.

Understanding a screen or a filter is to understand the language of the new literacy on which a new form of relationship to *otherness* depends. This relationship is not one of reciprocity or reception but of inclusion or exclusion. Everything that the screen exposes (or rather is expounded on it) is "the condition of existence" centered on the "*showable,*" in a way similar to what Berkeley meant by "*esse est percipi*" and then completed by Husserl as "[that] *est percipi qua percipi.*" The Husserlian modification brings together the ontological displacement operated by the Berkeleyan position—not sub-stantialist—with the certainty of the liveliness of the experience.

The screens present a world without walls, where there seems to be

---

[8] One of the newest experiences when visiting old buildings in France is to find oneself obliged to resort to screen devices as a condition of having a "real experience" of that visit.

no obstacle, where everything can be reversible, simultaneous, amplified, penetrated, knowable, transparent, but with forcefulness of the immaterial, which is therefore unlimited.

2. Ambiguity of Purpose: What Is the Screen?

The screen or filter allows access to phenomena around us by means of a collective awareness of them, while the realization of the resulting experience is poured into representations that are taken for real without knowing for certain whether they are real or are merely a reality revealed by the devices that expose it.

The logic of the devices *super*imposes the order of being on any other order of reality.[9] If the power of the negative is mediation, what follows as *in-different* continuity is a diffraction of consciousness, a kind of transit without resolution; alienation in oneself, in the false consciousness of oneself. The complement of the other disappears.

How is it possible today to achieve a synthesis between the one alluded to in itself and outside of itself or in another, as a return to itself, in the form of consciousness and meaning? Or, rather, is it a permanent outside of itself continuum of interrelations, which enables the polysemy of meanings?

While we experience an object, the consciousness is focused on this object; the rest of the world and the various objects are stored in our repertoire as something we believe to be the case but to which we do not pay attention. The same is true for most of the many inexhaustible features of any object. All these additional features of the object, together with the world that surrounds it, constitute what Husserl called the horizon of that experience. The phenomenologically internal horizon pertains to the various characteristics of the intended and mentioned object, while the relational world, to which other objects and their relations—including language—belong, constitutes the external horizon.[10] The screens have in themselves the capacity of the performance to "induce" in the ordinary sense of an inference mode that is "to go-further-there" (*hinauslehnen*)[11] It is not only the anticipation of determinations of objects of material experience or their representations, but it means that "they are new objects" literally.

3. The Problem of Representation: What Is the Screen?

The recognition of the other according to a supposed equality of being has been transformed into an institutionalized simulacrum, where the sciences are no longer thought of as a morphological correlate of what is. The validity of the prefix "trans-" alerts us to a displacement of psycho-cognitive isomorphism representing the other to install a relaxation in which the reality of otherness becomes standardized as a mere discursive

---

[9] Cartesian *mathesis universalis* plus Ilya Prigogine's work on thermodynamic systems as set out *La fin des certitudes* (1996) / *The End of Certainty: Time, Chaos, and the New Laws of Nature* (1997).

[10] Merleau-Ponty, Maurice. *Le monde sensible et le monde de l'expression : cours au Collège de France : notes, 1953*, Genève, Métis Presses, 2011

[11] German word used in theater to indicate "the fourth wall," where the stage faces the public.

enunciation.[12]

In the passage from phylogenesis to ontogenesis modeled by neuroscience, the human brain (neocortex) is the only one capable of discerning established hierarchies in relationships with others, with nature and the biosphere, and with itself (emotions, affections, self-perception). Current literacy needs to move away from emotions and affects to be effective in formal relationships whose matrix leads to the isolationism of hyperconnectivity. The extension of the central nervous system is conceived as a distinct continuity in each organic function and its efferents, whose terminals are the independent consciousness and the skin. The notion of relationality as the result of human capacity, proper to the species, to produce an objective image of the world is a presumption and pretension of classical phenomenology.[13]

The concrete body that was traditionally a reference of all possible interactions—though tacit or devalued—is dissolved as an impossible dehiscence of centrality, susceptible to new complex aggregations, increasing and de-creasing. Self-organization gives rise to the concept called *hologramathic*, generator of virtualities for multiple developments and applications. Within the social, this is articulated as self-producing interactions. According to Morin, by dispensing with the subject "all our vision of the physical world is done through the intermediation of representations, concepts or systems of ideas, that is, of phenomena of the human spirit."[14]

4. Paradoxical Ambiguity: Real vs Verification of the World. What Is Literacy in This Sense?

The natural system of science has been transformed into integrated internalization of all parts conceived as processes generated by the force of human activity (technological operations of knowledge).[15]

The screen has reversed the relationship between the modern natural science model, that reality is everything that can be observed directly; the screen is now the condition imposed on the observable. The real truth is all verification made through it. The reality is visible because the screen of the devices shows it and, at the same time, because it prompts what it should be by giving orientations about what has to be visualized, evaluated, considered, etc. It would be inaccurate to go on saying that screens display representations of the world; rather, they present reality independently of what the senses can attest.

Literacy within this context is manifested under the requirement of levels of reality that are linked unevenly and that are not uniform globally because there are areas of resistance.

---

[12] Morin, Edgard. "La epistemología de la complejidad [Epistemology of Complexity]" *Gazeta de Antropología*, vol. 20, no. 2, 2004, www.ugr.es/~pwlac/G20_02Edgar_Morin.html.

[13] Gurdjieff, G. I. *Views from the Real World: Early Talks as Recollected by His Pupils*. E. P. Dutton, 1973.

[14] Morin, Edgard. *Epistemología de la complejidad*. Gedisa, Madrid, 2008.

[15] For example. life is conceived as a dissipative structure and by aggregation with forms of life for which indeterminacy is the norm. See Capra, Fritjof. "The Crisis of Perception," *The Tao of Physics*, 1975.

The double screen represents the synthesis between scientific and philosophical thought deepening "the epistemic dynamic of forms."[16] However, it hides the complexity of understanding of what is true—of reality—by making it ungraspable, by its permanent mutability and ephemeral state. The scale changes that the double screen can display are only contributions to a fictional unit that uses the name of reality.

Paradoxically, the invitation to connect to the multiple screens offered uses emotional resources whose purpose is to excite the will to do so. For this they promise to see and feel more intensely or have amazing experiences impossible without recourse to the screen device.

However, it also requires from the central nervous system an over-qualification of attention on the device, so that the place visited will always be less interesting than what the screen itself displays or opens.

One may then ask what is real in this context of the appearance of meanings, since what is taken as material spaces of displacement or of immediate sensory-perceptive extension is not what the device screens record. In the case of the October 2018 exhibition of the *Conciergerie* of Paris, the value of the real journey through the historical space depended on what the application of the devices allowed the visitors to see while they moved. What was the purpose of conceiving that way of incursion to the emblematic building associated with the reign of the Luises?

The new literacy required is that which can be expressed in algorithms and equations, independent programs of every material or conceptual edge whose characteristics converge in the infinite reproduction of attributive configurations ("noesical" meanings) making possible the generation of a something (entity), technically cash, a condition not necessary or sufficient for intersubjective relationships.

Vous pouvez radiographier le corps, le corps peut être autopsié, le rendre aussi transparent qu'ils le veulent, mais ils ne verront jamais avec leurs yeux le secret de la relation sexuelle; ou plutôt, ils ne verront jamais la seule vérité qui fait sauter les yeux: qu'il n'y a rien à voir, qu'il n'y a pas de secret. (Wajcman 223)

CONCLUSIONS:

1. The central nervous system undergoes its amplification and extension through the interaction of the screens with each other. This could be said without the dynamics of the amputations provided in the MacLuhan`s tetrad.

2. The various existing screens are filters because they show only what they make possible, and what remains outside becomes incommensurable and therefore incomprehensible and chaotic report, almost *noumenal* or banal. Nowadays nobody wants to give up having access to everything, at all times and in all places, on their small screen. The smartphone has turned the whole world into an expert in multitasking.

---

[16] Hays, Susannah. *Nature as Discourse: A Co-Evolutionary Systems Approach to Art and Environmental Design.* 2016. University of California, Berkeley. Ph.D. Dissertation, pp. 15 ss.

3. The double screen is a concept that can be perfectly inscribed in phenomenology: if in any perception there will be some fulfillment, what the screen does is to compose a new *noematic mode*, which corresponds to what at this moment is the screen. The fulfillment of the concept occurs when a ported device shows something that is expected from reality while bursting dramatically, in the course of daily continuity, with images that the subject's central nervous system takes for granted as true or similar. But anticipation and fulfillment occur in different orders as it were: the fulfillment is of the order of being, which is to say that it exceeds the intentional[17] only as *signifying* and *significative* configuration, in the same way in which "the medium is the message." What is shown is what it is as concrete perception. The real objects (or properties, or relationships, etc.) of the world are known by the screens as existing within the temporal space horizon. This new awareness of reality requires autopoietic literacy, a necessary expertise that positions one to feel and experience creation as it happens—in its immanence and its variability—and puts subjects in the belief of their roles as the concrete doers or makers of the material fragments of their world. The dehiscence of the images is the mediatic condition of the dehiscence of the experience of experiences; the natural attitude ends up being the transcendent expression of experience. Repetition indicates the impossibility of connecting with the experiences of others or that every subject searches through the screen devices for new experiences of the predicted. The anticipation of disappointment with what we do not find in the sought-after experience makes it impossible to dispense with the screen, or filter, because without it we are condemned to live without reality, in the plain of everyday life, a *nuda vita* or naked life, without any hope of feeling the unprecedented in experience.

4. The dehiscence of the corporeal consists of making visible even the impossible under the mortal condition of making disappear the original motive that sustains the belief that the devices are capable of showing more faithfully what there is.

WORKS CITED

Capra, Fritjof. *The Tao of Physics*, University Press, N.Y., 1975.

Gurdjieff, G. I. *Views from the Real World: Early Talks as Recollected by His Pupils*. E. P. Dutton, 1973.

Hays, Susannah. *Nature as Discourse: A Co-Evolutionary Systems Approach to Art and Environmental Design.* 2016. University of California, Berkeley. Ph.D. Dissertation.

Husserl, Edmund. *Ideen zu einer reinen Phänomenologie und phänomenologischen Philosophie. Erstes Buch: Allgemeine Einführung in die reine Phänomenologie.* Halle: Verlag von Max Niemeyer, 1913. Freiburg: Albert Ludwigs Universität. freidok.uni-freiburg.de/fedora/objects/freidok:5973/datastreams/FILE1/content.

---. *Ideas Relativas a una Fenomenología Pura y una Filosofía Fenomenológica.* Translated by Antonio Zirión

---

[17]*Absichtlich Bewusstsein* in Husserlian terminology is to express the ecstatic exit of consciousness from the world.

Quijano, UNAM, Fondo de Cultura Económica, 2013.

Merleau-Ponty, Maurice. *Le monde sensible et le monde de l'expression: cours au Collège de France, notes, 1953*, Genève, Métis Presses, 2011.

Morin, Edgard. *Epistemología de la complejidad*. Madrid: Gedisa, 2008.

---. "La epistemología de la complejidad [Epistemology of Complexity]" *Gazeta de Antropología*, vol. 20, no. 2, 2004, www.ugr.es/~pwlac/G20_02Edgar_Morin.html.

Müller, Jens. "¿Qué es y cómo afecta la doble pantalla?" *Diario Las Américas*, 6 February 2017, www.diariolasamericas.com/tecnologia/que-es-y-como-afecta-la-doble-pantalla-n4114217.

Prigogine, Ilya. *La Fin des certitudes*, Paris: Odile Jacob, 1996.

Wajcman, Gérard. *L'Œil absolu*. Paris: Denoël, Paris, 2010.

Heidegger's Digits

LUANNE FRANK

UNIVERSITY OF TEXAS AT ARLINGTON
ARLINGTON, TEXAS, USA

ABSTRACT: *With the burgeoning of animal studies, Heidegger's understandings related to human and animal hands become important beyond what the simple coupling "Heidegger and the Hand" might earlier have suggested: Heidegger again becomes anathematized. Derrida takes up the oppositional cry in his "Geschlecht II," linking Heidegger to the monstrous and claiming that Heidegger's "long maneuver" concerning the hand "makes of the path of thinking and of the question of the sense of being a long and continuous meditation on the hand."*

If this is so, then to question Heidegger's understanding of the hand, as Derrida famously does, will mean to call into question Heidegger's path of thinking and thus cast a shadow over his groundbreaking attempts to answer his (and philosophy's) great question.

A recent essay, as yet unrefuted, Tom Tyler's "The Rule of Thumb," casts such shadow, arguing that Heidegger's understanding of the human hand includes an insistence on its structural uniqueness. Tyler thus identifies Heidegger as a sort of pre-Darwinian, one resembling a certain John Bell, a nineteenth-century believer in Divine design, who insists on a structural difference between human and animal hands.

A comparison between what Tyler argues as the meaning of Heidegger's understandings of the relation between human and animal hands and what Heidegger makes clear he intends suggests that Tyler's argument misses Heidegger's point. Tyler and Heidegger are speaking two different languages—Tyler, the metaphysical, and Heidegger the non-traditional ontological. Heidegger distinguishes the two in Being and Time. Heidegger acknowledges structural sameness between animal and human hands. His concern, though, is not structural. It is with the difference in capacity that separates hands that are structurally the same. The human hand can write. Tyler either misses this or evades it. Acknowledging it would render his argument irrelevant to Heidegger's concerns.

KEYWORDS: Heidegger, human hand, animals, digits

What follows questions an essay on Martin Heidegger that, oddly, finds him *justifying* an argument for humans' structural superiority to animals to support the claim of humans' right to world domination.

I take us briefly through the essay, then ask the bases in Heidegger on which it makes its assertions, and finally read what it quotes *of* Heidegger in a way Heidegger, if we understand him correctly, will himself have intended. This may be quite different from what the essay in question asserts. It and the Heidegger it points to have to do with human and animal hands and specifically with the nature and capacity of their digits. This being so, and humans' digits never more crucial to humans than now, Heidegger's insights here maintain a significance comparable —and related—

to those pointing to the meanings of being. This is so despite the shift of the current primary meaning of "digit" from finger or toe to the electronic manipulation of ones and zeros.

The question of Heidegger's understanding related to the hand becomes critically unavoidable when Jacques Derrida points out a basis for its importance in his "*Geschlecht* II: Heidegger's Hand," linking it with animal studies. We set Derrida's words there apart from *our* running text in the same way (framing them in space) as he sets apart *his* juxtaposition of Heidegger and the *monstrous* (161), to which his words on Heidegger and the hand relate. Derrida writes that Heidegger's "long maneuver" having to do with the hand, "makes of the *path of thinking* and of the question of the sense of Being a long and continuous meditation *on* the hand" (177).

To extend *Derrida's* observation: *if* Heidegger's path of thinking and his question of the meaning of Being, as well as his meditations on this meaning are indeed a continuous meditation on the hand, then to repudiate Heidegger's understanding of the hand will mean to call into question his path of thinking and cast a long shadow over his groundbreaking attempts to answer his great question.

A related essay, as yet unrefuted, casts such a shadow. Although its author, Tom Tyler, has written before, thought*fully*, on the question of how Heidegger holds the animal in relation to the human, here he reads Heidegger in a sense thought*lessly,* and in precisely the way that brought Heidegger to say, "science does not think." If Tyler's claims here are supportable in Heidegger's work, they mark important additional moves against Heidegger in contemporary scholarly campaigns for recognition of animals' rights and capabilities. Thus, it may be useful to look at Tyler's claims and examine the Heideggerian ground they focus on.

The essay in question, Tyler's cautionary "The Rule of Thumb," has to do with human and animal hands, as noted, and features evolutionary anatomical information about both that serves as Tyler's route to interpreting Heidegger's writings on the hand. Should Tyler have uncovered the understandings that, he argues, Heidegger intends, he will have shown—in the face of much evidence to the contrary—that Heidegger's thought, noting demonstrable human capabilities not vouchsafed animals, supports assumptions about special status of humans in the world and the rights it purportedly gives them.

With much thus clearly dependent on Heidegger's understandings, one asks: Does Tyler read them accurately? Does he reach as far as Heidegger? If not, we must follow as far as Heidegger's understandings might take us.

Beyond this, I call attention to Tyler's essay lest readers not yet familiar with Heidegger suppose Tyler's understandings definitive—this due to his essay's easy, mocking tone, suggesting his apparent conviction that his argument has crucial relevance to Heidegger.

Tyler's specific focus on Heidegger proper occupies little space in his essay—not, though, as if this focus were but momentary. The essay's contents up to the point at which Heidegger comes to explicit mention function as supports for precisely what will be said *of* Heidegger. When Tyler states he is going to "explore" what "the work of a nineteenth-century writer" "can tell us about contemporary understandings of the hand and thumb," he is already aiming at Heidegger (437). For the only *contemporary* representative *of* these "contemporary understandings" Tyler will ever name here, and about whose thought the nineteenth-century writer is to tell us something, will be one, and only one, of the *twentieth* century's key thinkers, here made representative of presumably numerous others—strategically *unnamed* others—a "those" to whom Tyler nonetheless points, whose views apparently parallel Heidegger's.

Before proceeding, let us note the preliminaries Tyler provides for these Heideggerian views by reviewing key aspects of Tyler's study. His essay is immediately appealing. It hooks us instantly, announcing its intention to demythologize—an intellectual sport in the West since Plato—and identifying three recognizable "rules of thumb": 1) permission to thrash one's wife if the rod is no thicker than a thumb, 2) the downturned thumb as indicative of the fate of a failed gladiator, and 3) the view of the human hand's opposable thumb as unique (435-47). With this, the word "unique" will haunt the essay, reminding of its focus, the third rule. To demythologize this rule as the basis of humans' self-aggrandizement is part of Tyler's purpose. Already labeled false as a description of the structure of the human hand with Tyler's first mention, the word "unique" nonetheless makes no fewer than five appearances in a still only introductory paragraph questioning humans' hands legitimation of humans' world mastery.

But the claim of the human hand's structural uniqueness, which Tyler takes pains to refute, had already been long disputed by Heidegger's time nor was Heidegger unaware of this.

Nonetheless, Tyler writes, those still exist who insist on the human hand as unique. To exemplify them, Tyler selects a pre-Darwinian, John Bell, a believer in Divine design (448) from whom he quotes amply (437-51). Then, as disproofs of Bell's assumptions about the human hand's uniqueness, Tyler tours accounts of numerous animal hands and hand-like appendages, putting to rest any supposition that structurally comparable hands are anything but ubiquitous and strikingly primitive. Not only are pentadactylic appendages traceable back some 365 million years, but some tetrapods who dragged themselves from the deep had 5, 6, 7, and 8 digits per limb. Moreover, specialization *diminishes* the number of digits (440). The champion of digital evolution is not human but the horse. Its appendages terminate in a *single* digit (440-41).

These accounts might have carried the day for this essay were its key point only the non-uniqueness of the human hand's structure and the mind-numbing extent of humans' lack of a guarantee of superiority to animals on this score. But Tyler does not stop here. He cites a conceptual distinction in comparative anatomy between analogy and homology made by a well-known Darwinian Richard Owen (442-44) and brings the already discredited pre-Darwinian Bell *back* into the picture in order to further repudiate Bell's views of human uniqueness by refuting Bell's probable repudiation of homology. How? Via Owen's distinctions, which are still standard, as Tyler does not say but we note a study in *Acta Biotheoretica* identifying homology—"the *same* organ in *different* animals under every variety of form and function"—to be "one of the most substantial concepts of all biology" (321, 317).

With this, Tyler adopts a label for Bell exposing him as even more grievously uninformed than before. The label: Ron Amundson's "taxonomic nominalist" (32-34). Taxonomic nominalists suppose that "species are individually created and therefore essentially unrelated" (443). For them, species "exist as distinct and *unique* entities in the world" (443); "similar organs in different species are [for them] never 'the same'" (443). With the authority of homology added to Tyler's accounts of the evolutionary forerunners and current near-equivalents of animals' and humans' digital arrangements—which demonstrate unequivocally that human and certain animal hands are homologically the same, that there *are* animal *hands*—the extent of poor Bell's anatomical blindness is clear.

But even *after* Darwinians' and later scientists' recognitions of the widespread existence of animal hands, according to Tyler, beliefs like those of taxonomic nominalists do not die out: "Traces of [their] *determinedly anti-homological perspective* persist in the writings of *those* who would separate, *absolutely*, the human hand from the terminal organs of all nonhuman limbs" (443, emphases added).

Who might these "those" be? None other than Heidegger: "Heidegger, notoriously, would countenance no relation between the human hand and other varieties of vertebrate appendage" (443). This fixes Heidegger in a class with the pre-Darwinian: "To the extent that *humanistic* thinkers [who remain nameless] insist on an absolute difference between species or between appendages, they exhibit a taxonomic nominalism as pronounced as Bell's" (444). Again, we note the persistent plural pronouns when the essay will provide but a single name: "[Their] denial of structural homology… precludes the very *possibility* of recognizing identity between [structurally similar and] similarly-located appendages in different species;" thus do they betray "[an] anthropocentrism sustain[ing]" the "prejudicial rule of thumb…[which] upholds Man as 'the ruler over animate and inanimate nature'" (444).

This claim is startling in view of Heidegger's comments in connection with the human hand, which neither state nor imply that it confers ruler's rights to its possessor and in view of which Heidegger's understanding of humans' assignment in the world is that of husbandman or custodian charged with the wellbeing of the world. This is clear from numbers of Heidegger's works. To name but three: "The Letter on Humanism," where the human is "the shepherd of Being," as well as *What is Called Thinking*, Part I and *The Question According to Technology*, in both of which the human can forestall world devastation. Such views mark Heidegger's philosophical contribution to the environmental movement, long recognized. Michael Zimmerman's innumerable environmentally-concerned works alone are cases in point.

What, then, are the bases of Tyler's claims? I shall ask two questions here.

The first: with what does he support his reference to Heidegger's notoriousness for "countenancing no relation between the human hand and other varieties of vertebrate appendage"? (444) He does not say.

But he appears certain *enough* that Heidegger is indeed notorious to leave uncited those critics whose writings effect this notoriety. Heidegger has long been taken to task by representatives of animal rights responding to his *Fundamental Concepts of Metaphysics*, where he finds animals "poor in world" (185-86). For this he is unlikely to be forgiven. But another source than animal rights advocates in general, one more specifically focused on Heidegger and the hand, could account exceptionally well for Tyler's choice of the word "notorious" to describe Heidegger's observations. This would be Tyler's illustrious [1] How is this? The French translation of Hölderlin's "Mnemosyne" had mis-rendered Hölderlin's "we are a sign" as "we are a monster" and had set Derrida thinking. The following two sentences framed by Derrida by means of juxtaposing and spacing them off from his running text, as earlier noted, make his point:

> We are going to speak of Heidegger/ We are also going to speak of monstrosity. (161)

Thus, Heidegger's notoriety.

My second question: what are the bases of Tyler's taxonomic nominalist label for Heidegger after he classifies him with those unnamed "humanistic thinkers [who], insisting on "an absolute difference between species or between appendages"—a claim that Heidegger does not make—"would forerunner in commenting on Heidegger and the hand, Derrida. Though quoting Derrida copiously five years earlier in "Like Water in Water," Tyler leaves him unmentioned here. He nonetheless appears to be echoing Derrida's comments on Heidegger and the hand. One hears them as largely the meaning of Tyler's reference to Heidegger's notorious views on the hand. For who else than Derrida has designated the sign (the word), the signer (human) *and* his least dispensable five-digited appendage (the hand), and is the thinker who collectively celebrates the difference of all three from animals and their capacities with the words "monster," "monstrous," and "monstrosity," jack-hammering these into his essay on Heidegger and the hand (thirty-six mentions in four pages) as labels that are "worthy of thought"?

countenance *no* relation between the human hand and other varieties of vertebrate appendage"? (443) What *has* Heidegger said to suggest the label taxonomic nominalist? Tyler provides two brief quotations, only two (444). The first from the "Letter on 'Humanism,'" where Heidegger notes that the "human body is something essentially [keep this word "essentially" in mind] other than an animal organism" (247), and the second is from *What Is Called Thinking*, where he finds the human hand "infinitely different" from mere "grasping organs" (16). Tyler reads the two statements as closely similar, linking the body's "essential" otherness to the hand and reading both this and the hand's "infinite" difference as "absolute," a word Tyler uses here four

---
[1] Derrida, see especially pp. 166-69, 174-75.

times to designate the difference he says Heidegger sees separating humans and animals (443, 444, 448).

When he interprets Heidegger's statements thus, Tyler has already pointed to the variety of examples noted above of non-human animals possessing what anatomists have long regarded as bona fide hands. It would thus seem that he *requires* no more than the two quotations he provides, to indicate a blindness on Heidegger's part, echoing Bell's, to long-recognized anatomical fact. For could the body of a man, sometimes indistinguishable on a dissecting table from that of a gorilla, indeed be seen as "essentially [as in 'absolutely'] other"? Could a human hand, structurally much like that of a chimpanzee (Tyler provides a drawing) be "infinitely" [as in "absolutely"] different" from it?

Structurally speaking, it could not. This is *Tyler's* point. Heidegger would agree. But Heidegger's comments on the human hand make a vastly different point, a point that Tyler misses. Or does he evade it? Certainly, Tyler stops short of Heidegger. How so?

Tyler and Heidegger are speaking different languages, languages that Heidegger unequivocally separates from one another in *Being and Time* and thenceforth—Tyler's, the metaphysical; Heidegger's, the non-traditional ontological. Nor has Heidegger failed to emphasize *his* language *as another* language *and another* thinking. Tyler seems willfully blind to this here though in an earlier essay he had cited Derrida's noting *precisely* this: that in *Being and Time* Heidegger "withdraws the question of Being *from* the metaphysical" (Derrida 168). Tyler's metaphysical language and thinking limit his concern here to a matter with which Heidegger has no issue, namely sameness of structure. Heidegger's ontological concern is not a difference of structure but rather a difference of ability *given* the sameness of structure, a sameness he acknowledges. Heidegger's concern is not taxonomic. How can we know?

By looking at his words. As is well known, Heidegger privileges a certain handful. "Essence," in its several forms, is one. The spaces of meaning that the word "essence" opens up in Heidegger's care are wide-ranging and densely populated. They require a three-page account in Michael Inwood's *Heidegger Dictionary* (52-4), three very different accounts in Parvis Emad and Kenneth Maly's introductions to their three major translations,[2] and an introduction plus four separate accounts depending on different contexts in Alfred Denker's *Historical Dictionary of Heidegger's Philosophy*.[3] Such is this word's variety of potential meanings.

Heidegger exposes in the word "essence" and its variants their capacity for gathering meanings that enlarge the range of his ontology. They are not limited to a rendering with which Tyler's metaphysical language *fixes* the word to point to "essential" as

---

[2] See Petzet's *Encounters and Dialogues with Martin Heidegger*, pp. xvi-xviii; Heidegger's *Phenomenological Interpretation of Kant's Critique of Pure Reason*, pp. xv-xix; and Heidegger's *Contributions to Philosophy: From Enowning*, pp. xxiv-xxvii.

[3] See page 25 for the succinct account; 160-161 "On the Essence and Concept of Physis"; 161-62 "On the Essence and Concept of Ground; 162-63 "On the Essence of Truth"; and 114-15 "Hölderlin and the Essence of Poetry."

an "absolute"-ness. It is not, of course, as if, linguistically, the word "absolute" could relinquish the meaning Tyler chooses. Metaphysical meanings do not disappear. Indeed, Heidegger notes that one must go *through* them to get to the ontological. But even *as* absolute, "essential" is not at all an expression here of difference of structure, as Tyler would have us suppose. It points to a *different difference*: difference of *use* to which the human and the animal can *put* the *same* structure.

Though my point just now is the resilience of "essence" and of the parameters of its meaning, in general "essence" points to aspects of Heidegger's understandings of the humanness of humans. In what Tyler quotes and avoids acknowledging, he points to the second of two key capacities, i.e., speaking and writing, with which Heidegger identifies this humanness—namely with the *use* of the *human hand's* digits that renders permanent the sounded word. The human hand can write.

In his *Parmenides,* Heidegger arrives at his most incisive understandings of the ontological meaning of this unique *capacity* of the digits of the human hand (80-81, 84-85). There he views writing as a concretization of language as the bridge across which the human speaks the world. A legacy of this capacity is the digital revolution of which we are speaking today.

Works Cited

Amundson, Ron. *The Changing Role of the Embryo in Evolutionary Thought: Roots of Evo-Devo.* Cambridge University Press, 2005, pp. 32-24.

Denker, Alfred. *Historical Dictionary of Heidegger's Philosophy.* London: Scarecrow, 2000.

Derrida, Jacques. "*Geschlecht* II: Heidegger's Hand." *Deconstruction and Philosophy: The Texts of Jacques Derrida,* edited by John Sallis. University of Chicago Press, 1987, pp. 161-96.

Heidegger, Martin. *Contributions to Philosophy: From Enowning.* Translated by Parvis Emad and Kenneth Maly, Indiana University Press, 1999.

---. "Letter on 'Humanism.'" *Pathmarks,* edited by William McNeill. Cambridge University Press, 1998, pp. 239-76.

---. *Fundamental Concepts of Metaphysics: World, Finitude, Solitude.* Translated by William McNeill and Nicholas Walker. Indiana University Press, 1995.

---. *Parmenides.* Translated by André Schuwer and Richard Rojcewicz. Indiana University Press, 1992.

---. *Phenomenological Interpretation of Kant's Critique of Pure Reason.* Translated by Parvis Emad and Kenneth Maly. Indiana University Press, 1997.

---. *The Question According to Technology.* Translated by William Lovitt. Harper, 1977.

---. *What Is Called Thinking?* Translated by J. Glenn Gray. Harper, 1968.

Inwood, Michael. *A Heidegger Dictionary.* Oxford: Blackwell, 1999.

Kleisner, Karel. "The Formation of the Theory of Homology in Biological Sciences." *Acta Biotheoretica,* vol. 55, no. 4, 2007, pp. 317-40.

Petzet, Heinrich. *Encounters and Dialogues with Martin Heidegger.* Translated by Parvis Emad and Kenneth Maly. University of Chicago Press, 1993.

Tyler, Tom. "Like Water in Water." *Journal for Cultural Research,* vol. 9, no. 3, July 2005, pp. 265-27.

---. "The Rule of Thumb." *JAC,* vol. 30, no. 3-4, 2010, pp. 435-56.

Zimmerman, Michael. *Heidegger's Confrontation with Modernity: Technology, Politics, Art.* Indiana University Press, 1990.

---. *Contesting Earth's Future: Radical Ecology and Postmodernity.* Berkeley: University of California Press, 1994.

Web 3.0 and the Web of Life. Attuning the Noosphere with (the Intelligences of) the Biosphere in the Context of the Anthropocene

PIETER LEMMENS

RADBOUD UNIVERSITY
NIJMEGEN, THE NETHERLANDS

ABSTRACT: *This article reflects on the future of the noosphere and the technosphere, i.e., the two inextricably connected anthropospheres that have been added to the Earth's biosphere and have become the defining geospheres of the Earth in what has been called the Anthropocene or the epoch of decisive human impact on the Earth system. Engaging with the work of Bernard Stiegler, Peter Sloterdijk, Timothy Morton, and David Abram among others, this paper argues for the need to attune the future techno-noosphere—concretized at the moment with the emergence of Web 3.0, artificial intelligence, big data, and the so-called Internet of Things—with the inherent intelligences and operativity of not only the biosphere or the 'web of life' but also the ethnosphere, so as to create a homeotic, i.e., a co-operative and co-constructive techno-noosphere that allows for genuine ecological coexistence on a future planet that will depend on the way it will be taken care of—or not—by humans who are themselves utterly dependent on the many non-human forces and residents of the planet.*

KEYWORDS: biosphere, noosphere, technosphere, digital media, Anthropocene

INTRODUCTION

In an interview published in 2012, the French philosopher Bernard Stiegler responds to the question what he means by his notion of ecology of spirit with the following:

> If we want meaningful transformations to happen in the future of the planet in terms of the climate, for example, individual behaviors need to be transformed. These individual behaviors must become more conscious, more attentive, more caring towards that which surrounds them. And they must turn that which surrounds them into an object of desire. This happens through an elevation of collective intelligence, *that is to say through a relaunching of desire.* (14)

For Stiegler, the ecology of spirit refers to the idea that the human spirit or mind is always dependent on and embedded in a technical environment that makes human thinking and reasoning—as both an individual and a collective affair—first of all possible. The human spirit or mind is fundamentally and from its very first beginning shaped, constituted, and conditioned by technologies, most specifically by what Stiegler calls *mnemo*technologies or what may also be termed media here. It always presupposes a technical *milieu* of the mind and the study of the interdependence and interaction between the mind or spirit and its technical milieu is what the ecology of spirit is all about.

Stiegler studies this ecology of spirit through what he calls an *organology*, based on the fact that all spiritual ecologies consist of constantly evolving configurations and articulations of three kinds of *organs* or *organ systems*: the psychic or psychosomatic organs of human beings, the many technical or artificial organs that make up the technical milieu, and the social organs or organizations that are formed through the articulations of individual psyches via the shared system of technical organs. These three organ systems, as said, constantly co-evolve through a threefold process of psychic, social, and technical *co-individuation*. Although all three individuation processes are of course equally important, Stiegler is mainly interested in the way the development or the individuation of the technical organs affects the individuation processes of the psychic and the social organs. Think here of the way digital network technologies have completely changed—and are still in the process of changing—both our individual life patterns and our collective enterprises in the last two decades.

It is within such ecologies of spirit that our individual as well as our collective behaviors are formed, cultivated and transformed. Currently this process is going faster every day due to a dynamic of permanent innovation constantly accelerating to such an extent that both individuals and collectives have increasing difficulty to keep up with the pace. Not only that, but the very characteristics of this innovation serve predominantly to increase the speed, codification, control, and calculability of information exchange. There is no need to elaborate in detail on what is behind this acceleration, which is nothing other than globalized capitalism that has annexed the global technical milieu of the mind to enable ever more and ever faster production of commodities and to create ever more consumption, which is to say ever more consumers, to satisfy its unconditional and today virtually sacred imperative of increasing profits. The most important commodity nowadays is maybe not so much anymore the information that is needed to grab and hold our attention—movies, videos, games, commercials, facebook postings, likes, etc.,—but human attention itself, which has become the ultimate metamarket (Stiegler, *Technics and Time* 2-3).

LIBIDINAL ECOLOGY

Now it is patently obvious, to return to Stiegler's quote from the beginning, that the individual behaviors he mentions are none other than the behaviors of us consumer subjects. And I explicitly say subjects because for Stiegler consumerism is a process of subjectivation, the still dominant process of subjectivation of our time. More accurately, it is a process of *de-subjectivation* or rather disindividuation, individuation being his Simondonian term for the more familiar notion of subjectivation.

Now what characterizes consumerist (de)subjectivation in Stiegler's view is that it is precisely *not* attentive to, *not* caring and in an important sense *not* conscious of what surrounds it. It is therefore also irresponsible, and not so much in the moral sense but foremost in being *unable* to respond. True care and true attention require that one has an *affective* relation to what one cares for and attends to; indeed, every object of real attention and every object really taken care of is an object of *desire* or of *love*. And that is what the consumer is unable to do since the relation of the consumer subject to its objects is generally not one of desire, according to Stiegler, but of drive, which is to say of craving and ultimately addiction (*La télécratie* 106).

As one of the few philosophers nowadays who still draw substantial inspiration from Sigmund Freud, for Stiegler there is a crucial distinction between desire and drive. With Freud, he understands the human psyche as constituted by drives, which are distinct from animals' instincts in that they have no particular goal. It is not nature but culture that gives humans their goals and this occurs through a process that Freud has called sublimation, through which drives are bound and deflected toward social and cultural investments and are as such transformed into desires. And whilst drives are typically short term and finite, bent toward immediate satisfaction and the devouring, indeed consumption of its objects, desires instead are long-term and potentially infinite, attentive and patient, feeding and augmenting themselves as it were through the cultivation of their objects (Venn et al. 337).

Thus understood, sublimation is a process of accumulating and directing what Freud called *libidinal energy*, which is the energy of the psyche, both individual and collective, and which expresses itself in all kinds of affective and cognitive or noetic dispositions like love, tenderness, passion and dedication or wonder, curiosity, puzzlement and the will to know. It forms the psychic potential of human intelligence, attention, and care in the broadest sense and is also very much a bodily thing. You can *feel* it running through your system in more or less subtle ways.

For both Stiegler and Freud, human civilizations are basically ways of capturing and directing the libidinal energy of individuals toward collective social and cultural goals and any civilization is as such a process of sublimation through which the egoistic energy of drives is transformed into non-ego-centered socialized and cultivated psychic energy (Stiegler, *Économie* 19-20; *La télécratie* 15). Sublimation thus gives rise to an elevation of the psyche, whilst what Marcuse later called desublimation causes a regression of the psyche in that it reverts desire back into drives. Now what crucially distinguishes Stiegler's view from that of Freud—and what I want to lay emphasis on here and explore in the current context of the Anthropocene as the age of planetary crisis—is that these processes of sublimation and desublimation as transformation of libidinal energy are fundamentally modulated or mediated by technologies, or let us say media in front of the present audience, and that means by a technical system or milieu of mnemotechnologies, indeed by an ecology of spirit, which must thus be understood in terms of an ecology of desire or a "libidinal ecology" (Stiegler, *What Makes Life* 71; *The Lost Spirit* 4, 77ff).

It is this intimate relation between desire or affectivity on the one hand and technology on the other, media technology especially, that Stiegler describes as "the artefacuality of desire" in *The Lost Spirit of Capitalism* (49) and explores in the second volume of *Symbolic Misery* as the fundamental link between desire as sublimation and *techne* (95), which is insufficiently, if at all, recognized today in philosophy of technology. Yet, to be mindful of this link is of the utmost importance in the current context of the Anthropocene in which the fate of the planet is becoming dependent on us humans *and* vice versa (Hamilton 5, 52), which means that our responsibility is called to rise to a whole new level, indeed that of the planetary. And this is the case because, as suggested by Stiegler, in the age of the Anthropocene it is the ecology of spirit—today an *industrial* and *digital* ecology as all global organological configurations are becoming industrialized and digitalized—that ultimately conditions any possibility of solving the problems in the ecology of nature.

We need to revolutionize our economies and our current energy dependencies, of course, but what we need primarily is a spiritual revolution, indeed a libidinal transformation of industrialized human behavior from a still dominant irresponsible and careless consumerism to a responsible and intelligent care-taking of our planetary *oikos* and a wholesome practice of what object-oriented eco-philosoper Timothy Morton has called "ecological coexistence" with all the other residents of the biosphere (*The Ecological Thought* 4). As such, the prime ecological crisis that needs to be solved is not that of the ecology of nature and the energies of *subsistence* that it contains (say the fossil energies) but that of the ecology of spirit, which is to say of libidinal energy or the energy of *existence* (*What Makes Life* 91), since it is there that the root of the problem lies. And this spiritual transformation has to be thought organologically for Stiegler and that is to say in concert with technological transformation.

Now Web 3.0 as the supposedly third digital revolution that will implement artificial intelligence and the Internet of Things into the existing World Wide Web can be understood as a new system of technical organs that will inevitably engender a new ecology of spirit. And, indeed, we should think about the kind of media literacy that is needed to navigate and thrive in it. However, and this is the claim that I want to defend and elaborate here, we should also think about the way in which the so-called Web 3.0 that is spreading around the globe now can be designed to support integrating humanity in a much more conscious, attentive, conscientious, and caring way into the much older web out of which humanity itself has sprung and on which it is still (and most probably forever) vitally dependent, namely the Web of Life also known as the biosphere. We should in a way combine media literacy with ecological literacy or "ecoliteracy" (Orr 1991, Capra 1993) or better yet a planetary or Earth System literacy. And although most of us have become quite media-savvy in the 21st century, we have barely started learning to read and understand our ecological and even less our planetary situatedness.

ENTER THE ANTHROPOCENE

This is particularly important in the context of the Anthropocene, in which it is no longer the case, whether we like it or not, that we are just one of the threads in the Web of Life. We have become, willy-nilly, the most dominant if not its determining thread, yet it is still true, and even more so now, that what we do to the web of life we ultimately do to ourselves. Our modern will to dominate and control nature has been mostly destructive of this fragile web that we called nature and therefore, as we now start to realize, self-destructive. This cannot go on, however; we need to educate ourselves in a very profound way in ecological thinking and this means at its most elementary, as Morton conveys in The Ecological Thought, to realize that everything on this planet is deeply interconnected (1) and therefore deeply interdependent (30). To live in a biosphere means to live together with many nonhuman others, biotic and abiotic, within a huge and infinitely complex "mesh" (28) that is also familiar to us under the name of Gaia, which is very robust but so thoroughly disturbed by human action now that it is becoming a threat to human survival. Contrary to what the word suggests, ecological thinking means realizing that the Earth is not—or at least not only and certainly not in the first place—our home. It means acknowledging, as the German philosopher Peter Sloterdijk has pointed out, that what the 20th century phenomenologists have called the "lifeworld" and considered to be the ultimate bedrock of human existence, should be rethought in terms of increasingly precarious "lifeworld-implants" in an earthly non-lifeworld (*Foams* 458-9).

Although many authors, in particular a quite vociferous group affiliated with the so called ecomodernism or ecopragmatism, approach the Anthropocene anthropocentrically as the human age, in which our species will sovereignly shape the future of the planet, I tend to have more affinity with those authors who emphasize the uncanny return of the Earth as a decisive, if not *the* decisive, factor in human affairs. The return of the Earth is something to be reckoned with from now on as the ultimate object—or matter—of our concern, though decisively *not* anymore as something silently pliant to our will but rather as something actively responding to our actions and yet *not* particularly concerned about us, humans. Whether those authors speak of *The Revenge of Gaia* like James Lovelock, of *Waking the Giant* like Bill McGuire, of an "intrusion of Gaia" as Isabelle Stengers does in *In Catastrophic Times: Resisting the Coming Barbarism* (43), of our planetary civilization's need for *Facing Gaia* like Bruno Latour, of the emergence of a *Defiant Earth* like Clive Hamilton, or of the "ecological trauma" of the "end of the world" as Timothy Morton does in *Hyperobjects: Philosophy and Ecology after the End of the World* (14-15), the mantra is invariably that the Earth is taking center stage and is putting our current modus vivendi radically into question, forcing us to fundamentally re-consider, re-orient, and re-design our lives under the conditions that *she* poses and that this *first of all* means *paying attention* to her, as Stengers pointedly puts it (45). *Struggling* against Gaia makes no sense according to Stengers (53), while struggling against capitalism's assault upon the Earth makes all the sense in the world, despite the fact that we all seem to be convinced, after Thatcher, that "There Is No Alternative." As Stengers assures us, "*We will always have to reckon with Gaia*, to learn, like peoples of old, not to offend her" (58). My immediate reaction to this latter clause is: why not also learn *from* peoples of old? But I will come back to this at the end of this article.

Despite my sympathies for the terra-centric view of the Anthropocene aligned with the work of authors such as Sloterdijk and recently also Peter Haff (2013) and David Grinspoon (2016), what seems to be downplayed or receives little serious attention in the diagnoses of the authors just mentioned—despite their obvious awareness that technologized humanity has brought about the current shift in the Earth System—is the fact that today's Earth is endowed not just with a litho-, atmo-, hydro-, and biosphere but also with a *technosphere* as well as a *noosphere* which animates and is in its turn animated *by* this technosphere. I will not relate here the fascinating origins of the notion of noosphere, which was introduced in 1922 by the French paleontologist and Jezuit scholar Pierre Teilhard de Chardin and adapted by the Russian geochemist Vladimir Vernadsky, but only observe that what is lacking in these earlier conceptions is an explicit linking of the noosphere to technology and that is to say to the technosphere. Yet, while these two meta-physical spheres (as I am tempted to call them) are co-original from a Stieglerian perspective, which theorizes the noetic as fundamentally enabled and conditioned by the technical and therefore thinks *noesis* essentially as *technesis* (*Symbolic Misery, Vol 2: The Catastrophe* 31; *Automatic Society* 132), I propose to talk explicitly about the *techno-noosphere* here.

The Techno-Noosphere

The notion of the techno-noosphere, I also want to suggest, may be considered a new way of thinking what Martin Heidegger started to call enframing or *Gestell* in the 1950s and what he already comprehended in the 1930s in terms of machination or *Machenschaft* as an explicitly planetary phenomenon (*Mindfulness* 13), though only in a strictly ontological sense and not as a truly geological or geophysiological sphere in its own right that would interfere physically, and that is to say thermodynamically, with the other geospheres. Be that as it may, such an Earth is very different indeed from the, let us say, pre-anthropic, biosphere-only Earth. As suggested by Sloterdijk, such an Earth may harbor unimagined potentialities that may drastically change the future prospects of human habitation as well as the flourishing of the biosphere at large, notwithstanding the fact that it is now the sphere that is depleting and deteriorating all the older spheres on which it fundamentally depends and is therefore still hurtling toward self-destruction (*Foams* 38).

Now, with this techno-noosphere, we are back with Web 3.0 as the emerging global ecology of spirit as it increasingly conditions the ecology of nature—the Web of Life—without ever being able to control the latter, of course, but nonetheless inevitably forced to start taking care of it—albeit in a still unimaginable and largely unfathomable way—and that is to say on penalty of rendering its very own presence within this Web of Life forever impossible. I agree with Peter Haff that the technosphere is the "defining system of the Anthropocene" ("Being Human" 103) and even more so that is it has become the *decisive* system within today's Earth System, i.e., the geosphere on which the future of the planet as a life-sustaining planet—and *a fortiori* of a *human* life-sustaining planet—now substantially hinges. Without going into the intricate and fascinating question of humanity's ultimate place within the technosphere, this assertion seems to put humans at the center stage again and conflict with the widely shared tenet that it is precisely our anthropocentric ideology that has been largely responsible for creating the global ecological crisis. This is without doubt true, yet the anthropocentrism of industrialized modernity was precisely an *irresponsible* anthropocentrism.

What is on the agenda of the Anthropocene, on the contrary, is the coming into being of a *responsible* anthropocentrism, interiorized by an *anthropos* that explicitly takes care of its earthly habitat based on the realization that it now has become, as Hamilton rightfully argues, the "*central agent on a new kind of Earth*" although an agent that is fundamentally "delimited by the newly activated and countervailing power of the Earth System" (49). Such a responsible, benign anthropocentrism may usher in what the American astrobiologist David Grinspoon has beautifully called the "mature Anthropocene," in which, as he writes in his book *Earth in Human Hands*, we would "fully incorporate our human powers of imagination, abstraction, and foresight into our role as an integral part of the planetary system" so as to switch to "conscious, purposeful global change from the inadvertent, random changes that have largely brought us to this point" (226).

It is true I think, as Hamilton writes, that the Anthropocene has burdened humanity with an unprecedented "amplified responsibility for the Earth" (53). This is where the ecology of spirit comes in again as that which increasingly conditions the planetary ecology of nature. To put it bluntly, we have reached a stage in which the human and the planetary history converge and where the fate of the Earth System as a (human) life support system is becoming dependent on human knowledge and desire conditioned by the global technical system of which the digital system of information and communication media, now evolving into Web 3.0, is probably the most crucial. And so, it is increasingly true, as Sloterdijk observed already in 1993, that "[t]he fate of the inhabitants of the Earth hinges today—more than in the age of cities and empires—on higher metamorphoses of the attention-coalitions" of mankind (*Weltfremdheit* 376).

When the noosphere is described as the feedback effect of the collective human attention to the planet, the prime focus of caretaking for our future planet is therefore *attention* in the sense of the awakening to a *new* attention, indeed to a whole new *level* as well as a whole new *quality* of attention—an attention carefully attuned to our planetary residence. And, in that sense, one can argue that for the moment the noosphere is still largely an ignoosphere—still only *in itself* but not yet *for itself*, to put it in Hegelian terms—because the majority of earthlings persist in what Stiegler has diagnosed as a "*global attention deficit disorder*" (*Taking Care* 57, 179), its libidinal energy captured, absorbed, and exhausted on a massive scale in the dispiriting and addictogenic media ecologies of global consumer capitalism.

This new planetary attention or consciousness obviously necessitates an elevation of collective intelligence, but I would argue that it first of all requires that the Earth become an object of affection and care, indeed "an object of desire" in Stiegler's terminology ("Interview" 14). And with that, he means an object of *collective* desire to be acquired by humanity on its way to becoming a planetary collective. Yes, we might even state that the Earth is to become the *ultimate* object of collective desire––the latter expression being Stiegler's postmetaphysical, libidinal redefinition of what in metaphysics or ontotheology was always called God (*What Makes Life* 78).

If the future of the planet now depends on humanity's collective libidinal energy, and if this energy is indeed shaped and modulated by technical milieus—first of all the mnemotechnical milieus that have now become overwhelmingly digital and constitute today's techno-noosphere—the big question regarding the emerging Web 3.0 and the new digital devices and algorithms it will implement (again: big data, artificial intelligence, ambient computing, machine learning, the Internet of Things, etc.), is whether it can eventually serve as the collective platform, the common instrument as it were, of this necessary awakening of planetary consciousness and care, of this elevation of the global libidinal economy or the "relaunching of desire" as Stiegler puts it in an admittedly somewhat awkward fashion toward a wholly new, planetary level ("Interview" 14).

WEB 3.0 AND THE WEB OF LIFE

I think it is not all that difficult to imagine that Web 3.0 could—and indeed *should*—evolve in the long run into a genuinely intelligent global techno-noosphere that will allow humanity, as a global collective, to engage in what Grinspoon describes as "intentional, deliberate interactions with the planet" (xv) or "self-aware global change" (262) in order to become a truly "planetary intelligence" capable of "more globally coordinated cognitive activity" (142) through which to take care of the planet. Indeed, it may evolve into a shared "mechanism for global control" (xv) that allows us technologically to acquire the totally unprecedented "global scale intention" (426) that is necessary for any intelligent future management and caretaking of the planet.

Web 3.0 technologies could evolve within this context into new "techniques of the self" and support new modes of "the care of the self" and others in the Foucauldian sense, but could now include non-human others and become as such "techniques of sublimation" (Stiegler, *Taking Care* 172) instead of only intensifying the now dominant trend of desublimation and regression into drive-based and careless behavioral patterns as they mostly do in the context of contemporary cognitive and consumerist capitalism. For Stiegler, the possibility for this is grounded principally in the pharmacological nature of digital technology—and of *all* technology for that matter—which points to its irreducible ambiguity and states that the now deeply toxic, i.e., denoeticizing and disempowering impact of the digital techno-noosphere can and must be transformed into a remedy through the invention of new social and individual practices around it.

However—and this will conclude my all too brief exploration of the relation between the emerging Web 3.0 and the Web of Life—it is less clear, I think, whether the digital, electronic, and essentially algorithmic technologies of Web 3.0 can also serve to support a cultural project that I deem equally important for an anthropocentric humanity and that is to (really) reconnect with the biosphere or the Web of Life *at the local and personal level and in a deeply felt, sensorial and intimate way*. It is increasingly recognized today that this web must be regarded as a *noosphere in its own right*, albeit obviously a *non-techno-noosphere*, i.e., a non-organological but organic noosphere, yet one that is definitely sentient and possibly also conscious in some sense.

I am less and less convinced that the new digital media, properly practiced as *noo*technologies, can also serve to re-weave us into the Web of Life and to support a planetary awakening in the sense of a deeply felt experience of our implication in a biosphere that we share with many non-human others. I now hesitate whether digital media can be the right means for such experiences of immersion—as I would like to call them—although, on a closer look, it all depends on the kind of immersion we are talking about or the aspects of the biosphere in which we are immersed that are taken into account here.

It seems far more plausible *prima facie* that intensified use of these media in the context of Web 3.0 will only increase our existential estrangement from the fact that we are fundamentally immersed in the biosphere. This increasingly precarious and uncanny situation has been recently described in Lacanian terms by Morton as the "symbiotic real," meaning the "ecological symbiosis of human and nonhuman parts of the biosphere," which is, of course, largely unconscious today (*Humankind* 1,13). The reason is simply that digitization is a further progression of what the first volume of Stiegler's *Symbolic Misery* identifies as "grammatization" of human symbolic comportment, realized first through writing technology, then printing, next analog mnemotechnologies, and now through the digital (53-6).

As the American eco-philosopher David Abram has shown convincingly in his book *The Spell of the Sensuous*, the invention of writing—and, in particular, the alphabetic writing that inaugurated and sustained first the Greeks and later the whole Western process of individuation (49)—has progressively separated Western humanity from its more ancient, orally based immersion in the natural environment that had, Abram shows, the character of a reciprocal relationship with the natural world that was basically animistic and closely resembled the "being-in-the-world" of most of today's indigenous, tribal communities (137).

Oral cultures live in an intimate sensory reciprocity with the "more-than-human-ecology" (Abram 22), while literate cultures have increasingly distanced themselves from meaningful contact and communication with nonhuman nature and this might be one of the crucial factors behind the global ecological crisis that is now reaching a point of climax. According to Abram, literate cultures are actually animistic still, but instead of experiencing the natural environment as expressive and alive, they are spoken to by the letters on the pages of their books, which is even more mysterious if you think about it. The animating interplay of the senses has simply been transferred from the enveloping biosphere to another, artificial medium, that of phonetic writing (131). Indeed, Abram writes that it has been captured under the spell of that "strange and potent technology" that is the alphabet (95). How much more potent, then, is the spell exerted by today's *digital* writing that possesses the power to keep us all glued to our screens day in and day out, confronting us with a sheer infinite and ever changing abundance of symbolic, visual, and auditory stimuli that permanently solicit our attention frequently to the point of exhaustion. And it has all the potential to further alienate us from our immersion in the biosphere.

On the other hand, it cannot be denied that it is precisely digital technology in the form of satellite imagery, computer models, and much more that allows us to experience, although in a very abstract way, such complex planetary phenomena like the carbon cycles or climate change and offers us the possibility of rigorously theorizing and accurately mapping the Earth in terms of a unitary system in the first place. But, indeed, this knowledge remains abstract and hardly helps, or so it seems, to attain what Thomas Berry describes as an "intimacy with the natural world," which seems a prerequisite for a modus vivendi on the planet that is mutually enhancing and truly caring (26).

When Morton characterizes the emerging "ecological thought" as the awareness of sharing the biosphere with "a multitude of entangled strange strangers" and emphasizes the "weirdness" and "uncanniness" of our newly discovered implication in a vastly complex biosphere, one could argue from Abram's eco-phenomenological perspective that these feelings of strangeness and uncanniness are easily explained by our deep estrangement from the biosphere as digitized postmoderns and by the fact that we have lost completely an intimate, sensorial attunement to it (*The Ecological Thought* 15, 53). Yet, interestingly, Morton also characterizes the ecological thought explicitly in terms of "*intimacy* with the strange stranger" (46, emphasis added). But *his* notion of intimacy does not pertain so much to beings that we encounter with our senses, as it does for Abram, but more to those that we can*not* perceive with an unequipped sensorium. Earlier oral and animistic peoples have never been familiar with the bacteria in our guts, the DNA in our cells, the ultraviolet light that burns our skin, the oxygen and carbon dioxide in the atmosphere, global ecological cycles, nuclear radiation, and all those other things to which Morton devotes his attention in *Hyperobjects: Philosophy and Ecology after the End of the World* like plate tectonics, styrofoam and plutonium pollution, global warming, and the human species itself. These phenomena are mostly products of technoscientific *explication*, to use Sloterdijk's term (*Foams* 66), and would never manifest in the original clearing opened up by our senses and symbolic-linguistic signification that the late Heidegger associated with natural nature. They only manifest thanks to advanced technology that opens up a technical clearing (*Foams* 77).

TOWARDS A HOMEOTIC TECHNO-NOOSPHERE

I assume that Morton's ecological thought wants us to awaken primarily to *this* clearing, to *this* biosphere, which is totally different from the phenomenal and sensorially experienced biosphere of Abram. And it is to an enhanced intimacy with and a more profound attention and attunement to *this* biosphere that the new digital tools of Web 3.0 might indeed contribute a lot although their usefulness is obviously restricted to those aspects of it that lend themselves to digitization. Possible examples are provided by real time biological, ecological, and geological big data profiles on things like biodiversity, ocean acidity, radio-activity, climate change, ecosystem, health and carbon dioxide levels accessed through apps, microbiome monitoring devices, ecological footprint monitoring and optimizing gadgets—in fact, all kinds of digital tools that keep us informed about our ecological immersion and allow us to monitor and calibrate our actions.

These technologies might thereby help to foster a new kind of *solidarity*—a term invoked by Morton in the title of his recent book, *Humankind: Solidarity with Non-Human People* (2017)—with the many strange, nonhuman residents of this symbiotic real. They would bring into being, organologically, a new and expanded, more ecological ecology of spirit and also a new, again more ecological libidinal ecology through which we could enable these other residents to play a more profound role in our technically conditioned psychic and collective processes of individuation. Such an ecology of spirit could make possible an ecological coexistence with the other residents of the biosphere in some, albeit limited, sense as "subjects to be communed with, not as objects to be exploited" (Berry x). It would make for a less anthropo-exclusivist noosphere and one much more attuned to the highly complex and still largely unknown biosphere, one that would allow for a genuine geo-ecological perception of the Earth in which we could truly experience our deep connectedness with all the other Earth residents and Earth systems and attune our lives to it.

Yet, I would like to claim in closing that the digital Web 3.0 technologies, which function on the basis of calculation and belong to what the Belgian philosopher of technology Gilbert Hottois calls the "technocosmos" and its operative relation to the world, are only of partial use in supporting us to become more ecological or helping us realize that we always already *are* ecological, as Morton likes to emphasize (*Being Ecological* 215). The way Web 3.0 technologies can connect us to the Web of Life has certain, specific characteristics, which we may call grammatological after Stiegler and that can be anything but exhaustive. They can never open us up to what Heidegger once referred to as "the essential fullness of nature" [*Wesensfülle der Natur*] any more than the objectifying stance of the natural sciences can (*The Question* 174) or, for that matter, no more than *any* "access mode" can (Morton, *Being Ecological* 18). With respect to the biosphere and *a fortiori* the Earth System at large, we have to acknowledge that despite all our advanced knowledge we are ultimately still quite ignorant about what it is all about.

On that note, finally, we should start acknowledging that the *noosphere* is much richer and stranger than we can imagine as we should recognize that it is also an *ethnosphere* (Davis 2) in which many very different anthropic access modes to the biosphere have been pursued and are being pursued right now other than the scientific or naturalistic one that originated in the West and is today by far the dominant one. The recent so-called "ontological turn" in anthropology, represented here by Philippe Descola's *Beyond Nature and Culture*, has started to take seriously these other interpretations or enactments of being-in-the-world such as animism, totemism, and analogism, which can be thought to result from different ecologies of spirit and thus different libidinal ecologies. Of course, it makes no sense in the age of the Anthropocene and the time of hyperobjects to revert wholesale to such indigenous ontologies, but when it comes to our future task of attuning the noosphere more with the biosphere and its inherent intelligence(s), we might do worse than taking inspiration from what those ontologies, which generally display a profound solidarity if not true community with the non-human others in their environments, have to offer.

A viable and truly geo-ecological Web 3.0 noosphere should therefore be one that is explicitly designed to be compatible, i.e., co-constructive and co-operative not only with the biosphere but also with the indigenous parts of the ethnosphere instead of further deteriorating or eliminating both. Only such a *homeo-*techno-noosphere, carefully attuned to the biosphere and respectful of the wider ethnosphere, could function as a viable support for the "global-scale intention" (Grinspoon 238) that is needed to take care of the planet without further aggravating the catastrophic "unintended consequences" that have been produced by the industrial or even the "agrilogistical" (Morton, *Dark Ecology* 7, 52) noosphere and have led to the Anthropocene in the first place. A truly "Wise Earth" (Grinspoon 159, 196) should accord its global scale intentionality with all the other earthly intentionalities and agencies so as not to blindly destroy long evolved ecological and ethnic wisdom but to intelligently and carefully cooperate with it. Web 3.0 should "enliven" (Weber 3) the Web of Life, not further liquidate and deteriorate it.

WORKS CITED

Abram, David. *The Spell of the Sensuous*. Vintage, 1996.

Berry, Thomas. *The Great Work: Our Way into the Future*. Three Rivers Press, 1999.

Capra, Fritjof, editor. *Guide to Ecoliteracy*. Center for Ecoliteracy, 1993.

Davis, Wade. *The Wayfinders: Why Ancient Wisdom Matters in the Modern World*. Anansi, 2009.

Descola, Philippe. *Beyond Nature and Culture*. University of Chicago Press, 2013.

Grinspoon, David. *Earth in Human Hands: Shaping Our Planet's Future*. Grand Central Publishing, 2016.

Haff, Peter. "Technology as a Geological Phenomenon: Implications for Human Well-Being." *A Stratigraphical Basis for the Anthropocene*, special publications of Geological Society, London, vol. 395, 2014, pp. 301-309.

Haff, Peter. "Being Human in the Anthropocene." *Anthropocene Review*, vol. 4, no. 2, 2017, pp. 103-109.

Hamilton, Clive. *Defiant Earth: The Fate of Humans in the Anthropocene*. Polity, 2017.

Heidegger, Martin. *The Question Concerning Technology and Other Essays*. Harper & Row, 1977.

Heidegger, Martin. *Mindfulness*. Bloomsbury, 2016.

Hottois, Gilbert. *Le signe et la technique. La philosophie à l'épreuve de la technique*. Aubier, 1984.

Latour, Bruno. *Facing Gaia: Eight Lectures on the New Climate Regime*. Polity, 2017.

Lovelock, James. *The Revenge of Gaia: Why the Earth Is Fighting Back and How We Can Still Save Humanity*. Penguin, 2008.

McGuire, Bill. *Waking the Giant: How a Changing Climate Triggers Earthquakes, Tsunamis, and Volcanoes*. Oxford University Press, 2012.

Morton, Timothy. *The Ecological Thought*. Harvard University Press, 2010.

Morton, Timothy. *Hyperobjects: Philosophy and Ecology after the End of the World*. University of Minnesota Press, 2013.

Morton, Timothy. *Dark Ecology: For a Logic of Future Coexistence*. Columbia University Press, 2016.

Morton, Timothy. *Humankind: Solidarity with Non-Human People*. Verso, 2017.

Morton, Timothy. *Being Ecological*. Pelican, 2018.

Orr, David W. *Ecological Literacy: Education and the Transition to a Postmodern World*. SUNY Press, 1991.

Sloterdijk, Peter. *Weltfremdheit*. Suhrkamp, 1993.

Sloterdijk, Peter. *Foams: Spheres III*. Semiotext(e), 2016.

Stengers, Isabelle. *In Catastrophic

Times: Resisting the Coming Barbarism. Open Humanities Press, 2015.

Stiegler, Bernard. *Technics and Time 1. The Fault of Epimetheus*. Stanford University Press, 1998.

Stiegler, Bernard. *La télécratie contre la démocratie. Lettre ouverte aux représentants politiques*. Flammarion, 2006.

Stiegler, Bernard. *Économie de l'hypermateriel et psychopouvoir. Entretiens avec Philippe Petit et Vincent Bontemps*. Mille et une nuits, 2008.

Stiegler, Bernard. *Taking Care of Youth and the Generations*. Stanford University Press, 2010.

Stiegler, Bernard. "Interview: From Libidinal Economy to the Ecology of the Spirit." *Parrhesia*, vol. 14, 2012, pp. 9-15.

Stiegler, Bernard. *What Makes Life Worth Living: On Pharmacology*. Polity, 2013.

Stiegler, Bernard. *The Lost Spirit of Capitalism: Disbelief and Discredit, Vol. 3*. Polity, 2014.

Stiegler, Bernard. *Symbolic Misery, Vol. 1: The Hyperindustrial Epoch*. Polity, 2014.

Stiegler, Bernard. *Symbolic Misery, Vol 2: The Catastrophe of the Sensible*. Polity, 2015.

Stiegler, Bernard. *Automatic Society, Vol. 1: The Future of Work*. Polity, 2016.

Venn, Couze, Roy Boyne, John Phillips, and Ryan Bishop. "Technics, Media, Teleology: Interview with Bernard Stiegler." *Theory, Culture & Society*, vol. 24, no. 7-8, 2007, pp. 334-41.

Weber, Andreas. *Biology of Wonder: Aliveness, Feeling, and the Metamorphosis of Science*. New Society Publishers, 2016.

National Identity, Documentation, and the Dialogical Self

Tracy Powell

Western Oregon University
Monmouth, Oregon, USA

ABSTRACT: *One of life's most elusive mysteries remains the origin of self and identity. The perceived self as a fragile yet resilient and tangible thing we attempt to define and embody has been the source of much confusion and ambiguity among scholars of philosophy and psychology alike. Is selfhood reducible to a core essence as suggested by Jamesian theory, which purports the self-as knower and as known? Or, is self a narrative composition of multiple selves housed within one body, each presenting itself as the situational context demands? A change in national status forces one to confront the dialogic self as it overcomes obstacles of ambivalence and participation. Identity defined through documentation potentially threatens the dialogic process of multiple self-narration as it more naturally befits the Jamesian notion of a single definable self.*

KEYWORDS: national identity, dialogic self, ambivalence, participation

Who am I? Perhaps one of the most perplexing mysteries mankind has sought to unravel is the question of self-identity. The psychological understanding of self as an elusive, fragile yet enduring and tangible-like *thing* people attempt to define and subscribe to, has been the source of much confusion and ambiguity. Is selfhood reducible to a core essence, as suggested in Jamesian theory which purports the self-as-knower and -as-known? Or, is self a narrative composition of multiple selves housed within one body, a plurality of voices that shift in accordance with temporal, contextual, and motivational demands? (Hermans, "The Dialogical" 249) Changing nationality will be used to illustrate the complex process of narrating a dialogic self as it overcomes obstacles of *ambivalence* (Harrist 91) and *participation* (Ashworth 82). Moreover, identity defined through documentation will be shown to potentially threaten the dialogic process of multiple self-narration as it more intuitively resonates with the Jamesian notion of one definable, recognized self.

Self, from its etymological origin, pertains to being one's own person, or possessing a sense of sameness. A psychological understanding posits the self as an individual person who acts as the object of his or her own reflective consciousness. Historically, it has been common in psychological epistemology to conceptualize the self as a core essence housed within an individual person, a single entity or objective 'me' which can be known (Hermans, "The Dialogical" 249; Hermans, "The Construction" 100; Hermans et al. 23). From this understanding has evolved the study of personality which assumes the existence of stable, core, identifiable traits. This paper will argue against a

Jamesian self and instead consider self-construction and self-change from the perspective of the dialogic self; itself a creation of the dialogical narrator which is "(a) spatially organized and *embodied* and (b) *social*, with the other not outside but in the self-structure, resulting in a multiplicity of dialogically interacting selves" (Hermans et al. 23). According to this perspective, it is through participation in social environments that we create and are created, thereby generating a multiplicity of *I* positions within the self.

THE DIALOGICAL SELF

According to dialogical theory of the self, a composite is created within the concept of the self of multiple *I* positions that attempt to peacefully co-exist, assuming they can be integrated without diametrical opposition to one another. The anchor, points of the self differ according to time and place, consequently the dialogical self is "socialized, historical, cultural, embodied, and decontextualized" (Hermans, "The Construction" 89). Just as William James explained consciousness as an ever-flowing stream of thoughts in his functional analysis of the conscious experience, identity too can be understood as the inner narrative that occupies the imaginal space behind our observed actions. Jonathon Adler observes that, "Narrative identity is the internalized, evolving story of the self that each person crafts to provide his or her life with a sense of purpose and unity" (367). As a function of temporal coherence, woven together is a rewritten past, a perceived present, and a projected future designed to provide causal and thematic coherence to the narrator.

The socially constructed self is the 'me' positioned at the center of experience; a psychological reality contextually rooted in biological and sociocultural evolvement (Markus and Kitayama 423). The self then is only in existence by virtue of others and is agentic in that it derives meaning through interacting with others. Culture is not a set of beliefs that reside within a person, but rather a set of patterns and ideas that is located outside of the person (Markus and Kitayama 423). The self as body, brain, and psychological tendencies interacts with and upon the sociocultural content of the residing environment which leads to its dynamic constitution.

However, in times of change—when adopting a new nationality, for example—there is the inherent threat of temporary meaninglessness and incoherence which can adversely impact a person's sense of *eudaimonia*. It is during this reconstructive process of narration when struggles can ensue between one's accepted and embodied self-voice, as it becomes temporarily suspended without clear definition. At times of personal questioning, we can turn to tangible markers for reassurance of our identity—gender, age, educational background, marital status, and nationality being some prime examples. However, reliance upon such labels can stifle an otherwise healthy psychological moratorium of self-discovery (Erikson 157) thereby prematurely curtailing the development of further *I* positions with the self. Adler contends that it is through "living into" one's new narrative position that a sense of agency will ensue, which eventually will serve to restore equilibrium and promote psychological well-being (368). Thus, the unknown must be entertained for some while during which new *I* positions become incorporated into one's inner self narration.

Cultural transition can also be impeded when reification insulates pre-existing group membership from outside infiltration. As Hermans and Kempen explain, a tendency towards cultural reification can lead to false dichotomies such that "[p]eople turn names into things and endow nations, societies, and cultures with the qualities of internally homogenous and externally distinctive objects" (Adams and Markus 284). Thus, one might conceive of "American" as a static homogenous group identity versus something more fluid and heterogeneous; consequently, assimilation into the group is made more problematic by seemingly rigid group definition.

Adams and Markus further suggest that culture is embedded within the explicit and implicit patterns that come to be associated with groups. As such, a person need not be a member of a particular group (e.g., American citizen) in order to engage in and be shaped by group patterns. Instead, simple awareness of such patterns is sufficient to enable participation. Aughey posits that national allegiance need not actually play a pivotal role in terms of self-definition. Rather, "[i]f identity is concerned mainly with selfhood—what one feels oneself to be—allegiance involves a sense of authoritative political obligation" (Aughey 337). Thus, while allegiance implies a legal obligation to the laws and practices of the adopted nation, it does not "require subscription to a nationalistic, common purpose" (Aughey 339). While allegiance requires a willingness to follow and live within constitutional rules, this differs experientially from an embodied feeling of love for one's country, or so-called patriotism. Allegiance embodies a shared ownership of something outside of us rather than a similarity of something inside of us (Aughey 339).

However, when uncertainty surrounds what the implicit or explicit patterns are within a newly acquired cultural identity, new members may at times retreat to the familiarity of prior self-positions. Successful group integration thus requires effort and motivation on the part of the out-group member (Amiot et al. 806) Coping and adaptation strategies in line with inclusion efforts must be present in order to harmoniously bridge the divide between the in- and the out-group members. Strategies of disengagement would sabotage any efforts at authentic group inclusion and potentially lead to further alienation thereby compromising psychological well-being and causing *social loneliness* (de Jong Gierveld et al. 486).

Acculturation also requires an acceptance into patterned behaviors on behalf of the welcoming group members. Thus, one can only become American if treated as such and accepted as such by the participating in-group members. As Ashworth explains:

> [f]rom the point of view

of members of the group, the newcomer, novice, alienated person, or wet blanket appears (i) disquietingly 'objective' (in the sense of addressing the taken for granted with a scrutinizing gaze of appraisal) and (ii) of doubtful loyalty (in the sense of lacking the appearance of shared commitment to the group which questioning acceptance of the taken for granted recipes tends to signal). (94)

Consequently, challenges exist on both sides, for the newcomer who acts to preserve her authentically-experienced self while simultaneously attempting to embrace or at least mimic a new group identity and for the existing group members who wish to preserve and protect their solidarity through strict adherence to ritualized normative behavior and exclusionary practices.

Popular television media has dramatized the above mentioned group dynamic as experienced by those undergoing the process of changing nationality. In the television sitcom *How I Met Your Mother*, the Canadian character of Robin, who currently resides in the United States, is paying for her coffee at the iconic Canadian Tim Hortons ("Duel Citizenship"). After a brief exchange with the cashier, the server comments, "Oh sorry, you're American. Here's your change." To which Robin adamantly replies, "I'm not American." In response, the server retorts with eyebrows raised in an accusatory tone, "American money? Didn't watch the Leafs' game? No please or thank you for the coffee? You sure don't seem like a Canadian." This exchange clearly illustrates the level of tension between the opposing characters as they defend their in-group characteristics and attempt a separation through their derisive comments.

What happens when the new identity arouses feelings of ambivalence as illustrated in the dialogue above? Such situations are not uncommon when changing national status, particularly if one status is to replace another rather than co-exist alongside it. Depending on the country, sometimes only one citizenship is recognized which means abandoning one's former national identity, at least on a public level. Important legal identification, such as the passport, now identifies one as something or someone with whom there is no historical or emotional attachment.

PARTICIPATION

Ashworth explains *participation* as a taking part in or sharing in something with someone suggesting that the lived experience of social interaction requires a communing experience. It is a non-cognitive way of being, existing as its own lifeworld with its own system of meaning (Ashworth 89). Thus, in order to fully participate, an emotional and motivational attunement to the new group's concerns on both an extrinsic and intrinsic level must exist. However, this process may be hindered when a person is unaware of the group's implicit knowledge, thus causing a retreat to better known *I* positions. Since "many of the group's own presuppositions are not conscious, and so cannot be elucidated for the newcomer ... [it makes] it virtually impossible for a welcoming group to deliberately lessen the mismatch between their ways of thinking and the newcomer's" (Harrist 17). Moreover, if the individual holds a commitment or attachment to a former group identity, this too can create an *ambivalence* towards new group membership (Harrist 17). Thus, in order to participate, the individual must gain some implicit understanding by communing with the in-group as well as valuing what the group values. But, neither of these practices can threaten self-definition on the whole, such that the person feels fraudulent or disloyal in her behavior.

Markus suggests that cultural adoption is an active process that requires participating in customs, values, and rituals of the country in which one resides. One can acknowledge a cultural event such as Independence Day in America, for example, even though one might feel inauthentic in celebrating it since a shared implicit resonance with the event's inherent meaning is missing. If we examine acculturation within this context, Hermans suggests that within the voiced self are multiple layers comprising early familial experiences and indigenous culture (Hermans, "The Construction" 95). When the introduction of new voices causes a clash between the personal and social positions, a situation not uncommon to acculturation, confusion, or conflict can ensue. Hermans observes that cultural

> [v]oices ... of origin do not simply disappear when people are involved in an acculturation process. Instead, the older or deeper voices are often established parts of the self, and they are challenged, evoked, repressed, or simply ignored when the person enters into a host culture populated by different and often dominating voices. ("The Construction" 95)

Hence, one voice becomes silenced at times when another voice assumes greater presence. This understanding negates the often painful struggle experienced in living between cultures and assuming that one must reach a single self-identity. Instead, a dialogical self assumes a collection of cultural voices that function as social positions within the self. As a result of the self being able to broaden itself by including less familiar *I* positions, the boundaries between the self and the non-self widen and decentralize allowing an *identity-in-difference* organization. Cultural boundaries are not erased; instead, they become exceedingly permeable as various cultural identities co-exist.

NARRATED DIALOGIC SELF

In order to restructure and reorganize a situated dialogical self through acculturation, three processes are said to occur (Hermans, "The Construction" 109-111). First, when a new position is introduced and accepted into the system, it enters into dialogue with the existing *I* positions. Second, a shift occurs within the system so that voices that were previously in the foreground move to the background. Third, the positions exist together as a cooperative subsystem in the self. By way of example, Hermans tells of a

Pakistani-American woman who shifts between her voices, explaining that her classmates do not think she is American enough, while her parents think she is too Westernized. He suggests that despite their discordance, there is enough symmetry in these two voices so that "a symbiotic relationship of ambivalence" is created enabling each to live off the other in a dynamic loop through means of mutual negotiation (Hermans 111). One does not necessarily have to be one or the other; rather, both voices co-exist despite their apparent narrative juxtaposition and each surfaces in response to particular situational demands. In essence a hybrid identity is constructed with autonomous *I* positions that gain relevance in response to contextual and temporal demands.

CULTURAL ATTUNEMENT

Can feelings of ambivalence (*ambi* attraction; *valence* aversion) regarding identity be overcome to an extent sufficient to empathize with a new collective consciousness? (Harrist 87) Ambivalence relates to psychological conflict evidenced in anxiety and impaired decision making and is common to the human experience (Harrist 88). It can appear inconsolable when confronted with oppositional views, thus resulting in "feeling torn" between sides. For example, when group identification is not voluntarily chosen, feelings of ambivalence can ensue which lessen the possibility of emotional attunement to the new group. Moreover, "when group members feel that some of their pre-existing identities are threatened by a change and that the new identity to be integrated 'pushes' aside these identities, it [will] be more difficult for the new identity to become integrated within causing conflicts within the self" (Amiot et al. 821-822).

Three shifts have been suggested to occur in the process of overcoming ambivalence (Harrist 99). First is *disorientation*—experienced as a sense of loss or disequilibrium accompanied by psychological angst; confusion results in feeling disconnected and uncertain, often torn by incompatible thoughts or desires. Second is *exploration*—the gathering of information to reduce disorientation; cognitive processes such as comparing and contrasting, weighing pros and cons, questioning, and procuring judgments, are all used as means to secure movement towards a particular direction and resolve feelings of disequilibrium. Third is *resolution*—the continued movement towards alleviating ambivalence; a reconciliation between contradictory pathways allowing forward movement and promoting change, a process itself requiring patience and tolerance. The pathway between these three elements of ambivalence is not necessarily linear, therefore the individual often fluctuates back and forth between various *I* positions, sometimes finding no resolution.

Returning to the television sitcom, *How I Met Your Mother*, Robin faces a legal dilemma that can only be rectified through her change in national status. Emotionally torn and ambivalent in her decision, she laments after a drunken evening at the Hoser Hut, "I'm Canadian. I always will be." Feeling simultaneously separated from her country of origin and yet not a part of her country of residence, she despairs, "I don't belong. It's like I don't have a country" ("Duel Citizenship"). Robin experiences a loss of belonging which translates into a lack of self-definition. In such instances, one could seek out legal identifiers such as a birth certificate, certificate of nationality, or driver's license, through which to garner acceptance, but what if these documents are incongruent with the currently embodied self? International travel writer, Julian Smith, describes the experience of relinquishing his passport as "a strange floating sensation, as if in some way I exist" (276). Labels of nationality inscribed in legal documents prove who we are and that we belong. Being without a clear label is like being without a passport—unidentified and anonymous even to oneself.

Concluding Thoughts

Buddhist teachings on the impermanence of the self espouse the notion that "[a]ll that we are arises with our thoughts" (Newland). Is the ambivalence experienced in embracement of a new cultural identity a conscious choice? Perhaps, when it is perceived as a choice between relinquishing one's former national identity in favor of another. This internal struggle can be tempered however in adoption of the dialogic self since it enables a "double allegiance" wherein both national identities exist as simply different self-positions which assume more or less relevance in accordance with temporal and situational demands (Aughey 336). The issue of emotional and cultural attunement may remain, as often a "depth and resonance" exists with only one national identity (Aughey 338). Nevertheless, in order to create a sense of eudaimonic well-being in times of change, acceptance of multiple self-positions need occur thereby allowing a shift (rather than an abandonment) between fluid symmetrical *I* positions as social context necessitates. Self and culture are dialogically entered into positions meditated by travel and translocality which result in hybrid combinations of multiple identities (Hermans, "The Dialogical" 253). Adopting an internal dialogical self enables one to dwell within a peaceful co-existence in multiple cultural identities, each experienced differently, as one narratively lives within their dynamic social realities. I am not one core self, but rather a dynamic constitution of selves that arise and function in response to contextual demands. I am neither here nor there but, rather, I am everywhere.

Works Cited

Adams, Glenn, and Hazel Rose Markus. "Culture as Patterns: An Alternative Approach to the Problem of Reification." *Culture and Psychology*, vol. 7, no. 3, 2001, pp. 283-296.

Adler, Jonathon M. "Living into the Story: Agency and Coherence in a Longitudinal Study of Narrative Identity Development and Mental Health over the Course of Psychotherapy." *Journal of Personality and Social Psychology*, vol. 102, no. 2, 2012, pp. 367-389.

Amiot, Catherine E., Deborah J. Terry, Dian Wirawan, and Tim A. Grice. "Changes in Social

Identities over Time: The Role of Coping and Adaptation Processes." *British Journal of Social Psychology,* vol. 49, 2010, pp. 803-826.

Ashworth, Peter D. "The Meaning of Participation." *Journal of Phenomenological Psychology,* vol. 28, no. 1, 1997, pp. 82-103.

Aughey, Arthur. "National Identity, Allegiance and Constitutional Change in the United Kingdom." *Nations and Nationalism,* vol. 16, no. 2, 2010, pp. 335-353.

de Jong Gierveld, Jenny, Theo van Tilburg, and Pearl, A. Dykstra. "Chapter 26: Loneliness and Social Isolation." *The Cambridge Handbook of Personal Relationships,* edited by Anita L. Vangelisti and Daniel Perlman, Cambridge University Press, 2006, pp. 485-500.

"Duel Citizenship." *How I Met Your Mother,* created by Carter Bays and Craig Thomas, written by Chuck Tatham, directed by Pamela Fryman, season 5, episode 5, CBS, 19 October 2009.

Erikson, Erik H. "Reflections on the Dissent of Contemporary Youth." *International Journal of Psychoanalysis,* vol. 51, 1970, pp. 11-22.

Harrist, Steve. "A Phenomenological Investigation of the Experience of Ambivalence." *Journal of Phenomenological Psychology,* vol. 37, no. 1, 2006, pp. 85-114.

Hermans, Hubert J. M. "The Dialogical Self: Toward a Theory of Personal and Cultural Positioning." *Culture Psychology,* vol. 7, no. 3, 2001, pp. 243-281.

Hermans, Hubert J. M. "The Construction and Reconstruction of a Dialogical Self." *Journal of Constructivist Psychology,* vol. 16, 2003, pp. 89-130.

Hermans, Hubert J. M., Harry J. G. Kempen, and Rens van Loon. "The Dialogical Self: Beyond Individualism and Rationalism." *American Psychologist,* vol. 47, no. 1, 1992, pp. 23-33.

James, William. The Principles of Psychology (1). London: MacMillan, 1890.

Newland, Tahlia. "We Are What We Think: The Full Quote and Commentary." Tahlia Newland, www.tahlianewland.com/we-are-what-we-think-full-quote/. Accessed 30 June 2019.

Markus, Hazel Rose, and Shinobu Kitayama. "Cultures and Selves: A Cycle of Mutual Constitution. *Perspectives on Psychological Science,* vol. 5, no. 4, 2010, pp. 420-430.

Weiss, Robert S. *The Experience of Emotional and Social Isolation.* MIT Press, 1973.

Surveillance through Gaze:
Moralistic Self-Presentation and Mediated Behavior

Tracy Powell

Western Oregon University
Monmouth, Oregon, USA

ABSTRACT: *Surveillance has become a phenomenon of renewed global attention and critique as news and social media outlets promulgate claims about a former U.S. President and his Administration surreptitiously wire-tapping the Office of the current U.S. Administration. A breach of privacy such as this is condemned when implemented unlawfully, yet we all live under a constant gaze of observation intended to evaluate and control compliance of our actions. How does one reconcile the experience of being watched under the proverbial microscope while simultaneously being the watcher of others? Effects of observation on the psyche and the manifestation of those effects on the authentic, morally driven, and overt behavior through mediated self-presentation is considered. Surveillance as a tool is examined for its role in helping discern truth as authenticity within persons and across situations.*

KEYWORDS: gaze, surveillance, authenticity, social compliance

"Whenever you do a thing, act as if all the world were watching."
—Thomas Jefferson

Surveillance has become a phenomenon of renewed global attention and critique as news and social media outlets promulgate claims like those about the former U.S. President and his Administration surreptitiously wire-tapping the Office of the current U.S. Administration. Such invasion of privacy is something balked at when abused, yet we all live under an umbrella of observation and evaluation intended to determine and control the appropriateness of our actions. How does one experience being *watched* under the proverbial microscope, while simultaneously being the *watcher* of others? This paper explores the effects of observation on the psyche and its questionable manifestation in authentic, morally driven overt behavior through mediated self-presentation. Surveillance as a tool will be examined for its impact in helping discern *truth* as authenticity within persons and across situations.

The Watcher Is Watched

I watch myself
watch myself
watching their dance,
my action is actioned
by panel and plan

Significant thought
to trivial task,
I find myself missing

that which I've hatched

Impromptu I can do,
in scrutinies stare,
replayed ad infinitum
pretend I don't care

When waiting has waited
and I dare to break free,
will the watcher be waiting
or will I be free?
—Christopher Withers

On some level we are always under surveillance whether real or imagined, known or incognizant. The word's etymology indicates that the term surveillance had become used to signify a monitoring of "the actions and movements of suspect persons, outsiders, and dissidents" ("Surveillance"). As defined by Dictioary.com, surveillance is "a continuous observation of place, person, group, or ongoing activity in order to gather information." Mindful appreciation of the likelihood of such observation can impact the manner of our dialogue, behavior, and outward appearance such that we adjust our self-performance in response to ever-changing, culturally driven social demands. The accuracy of such observations and the information gleaned is deemed important for the efficient, lawful maintenance of any society.

Questions of authenticity and verifiable *truth* plague today's media under the guise of fake news in a manner perhaps unprecedented. Attempting to uncover the truth in spoken word, visible action, and written tweets has become an all-consuming, exhausting daily endeavor for providers and receivers of information alike. Media literacy has become of paramount importance to our cultural conscience which has been thrown into a chaotic state of uncertainty. As citizens we demand transparency of the reasons behind decisions made by those entrusted to protect and defend our democracy. But how do we know with any given certainty that what we are witnessing, whether through surveillance camera footage or videotaped interview, is factually accurate? How do we know that we are not deceived by media-manipulated images displayed on screen in the same way that an adept magician deceives us through illusion?

THE EYE

Let us take a moment to consider the mystique and allure attributed to the vestibule through which gaze is possible—the eye. This organ holds universal mythical and metaphysical significance historically and cross-culturally. For example, in the Sanskrit tradition the third eye represents a window to self-enlightenment and self-transcendence, whereas in Egyptian mythology, the evil eye casts an evil spell on those whose gaze it falls upon and leads to sterility and death (Berger 1099) and is similar to Medusa's imprisoning gaze in Greek mythology. Perhaps the most notable example of the eye's powerful gaze is captured in a description of the omniscient Almighty, the ultimate observer of behavior whose objective is to inspire and command moral righteousness through fear of retribution.

In the human emotion of love, we search one another's eyes for some glimpse into the truth they reveal, a reflection of endearment, desire, or commitment. It is within this gaze that we find and hold intimacy with another transcending the body to allow entrance to that which lies behind the surface. Conversely, in the emotion of hate, we encounter an angry gaze thought to initiate neural circuity and triggering our most visceral reactions in response to our threatened survival (Panagopoulos and van der Linden 114).

Everyone has experienced the feeling of unwanted eyes upon them; that heightened experience of being examined. As you become acutely aware of your conspicuousness, a prickly sensation spreads across your skin while an uncomfortable warmth settles within. With quickened heartbeat and moist palms you literally feel the eyes boring into the back of your skull, and a sinking feeling lodges in the pit of your stomach. The power of disembodied gaze, no less palpable than the pain of a phantom limb, creates this acute sensorial experience.

Gaze

Your glare weathered my cocoon
Leaving pores within my walls
So with each palpitation
My thoughts bled out
i remain an empty shell till
U return the substance
sustaining ur ego
And refrain from abusing my
  Fervor
  —Joe Perez

Whether beholden to favorable or cataclysmic purpose, the eye is thought to emanate an ominous force and impact through its receptive and projective qualities. One might consider artificial surveillance cameras as a technological manifestation of the all-seeing eye whose intent is to document and thwart unwanted behavior. "Big Brother" is a term synonymous with such governmental practice, as demonstrated in this excerpt from Orwell's classic *1984*:

> [t]he black mustachioed face gazed down from every commanding corner. There was one on the house-front immediately opposite. BIG BROTHER IS WATCHING YOU, the caption said, while the dark eyes looked deep into Winston's own. (Orwell 4)

Measures of surveillance are often met with resistance, veiled as intrusive, unwelcome invasions of privacy and sociopolitical oppression. Yet, ironically, current popular media trends reveal a heightened interest in such snooping behavior as witnessed in the popularity of reality television. Research reveals that reality media programming satisfies a psychological voyeuristic human curiosity (Baruh 192). The TV program *Big Brother* is one such example, where viewers peer in on "The House" and discern the moral rectitude of the inhabitants therein. Similarly, people watching is another guilty pleasure that allows for secret observation and judgment of others. Much less covert, users of Facebook, Instagram, Twitter, and other social media platforms openly display their lives for others to see and envy, being careful not to post information that would cast them in an unflattering light. Thus, in many instances we willingly engage in practices of surveillance and observation as much for entertainment as to inform our own humanity.

Media Surveillance

Ascertaining truth in media presentations is a central aspect of message comprehension. What is reality versus fiction, scripted artifice versus honest candor, or complicit contrivance versus unbiased reporting? With cameras capturing every moment and readers scrutinizing word choice down to semantic exactitude (e.g., President Trump's infamous tweet of the term *covfefe*), how does such mediatization impact one's decision to behave truthfully in accordance with one's authentic self?

Consider a person with antisocial personality disorder driven by narcissism who chooses to charm or revile based the agendas of the moment or a chameleon whose behavioral presentation fluctuates opportunistically (Hare 38). How do we determine what and who is his authentic self? We have heard repeatedly of requests for the President of the United States to be more presidential in his manner and to tweet his vitriolic, impulse-driven comments less frequently. Yet, those who know him well suggest that such control is not within his purview. He is enslaved by his own flawed personality and affectations. But is he? Or, is he manipulating his audience by choosing to revile with his frequently thoughtless tweets? Keeping us, his viewers, poised on tip-toe awaiting his next strategic move like pawns on a chessboard.

Who is the real Donald Trump—tactless political novice or an ingenious charlatan? The decision reached depends on the appraisal of the watcher—the lens through which his actions are seen, judged, and verified.

Psychological research on the *spotlight effect* has demonstrated that we moderate our behavior to fit our circumstances and the audience to whom we are attempting to influence or gain favor. The self, like a woven tapestry, has many threads, intertwined yet separate in complicated, creative patterns expressive of both transparency and concealment and seldom reducible to one core motif. Accordingly, Cooley's *looking-glass* self (Willis and Silbey 443) suggests that we are bound by an inescapably reciprocal outward-inward gaze of imprisonment, such that the self that prevails in any given circumstance—a *cosmopolitan self*—is little more than a fleeting social construction (Christensen and Jansson 1483). Since the egocentric delusion of an *imaginary audience* results in our continuous performance of selves, it behooves us to be mindful then of which self to present. Even alone, this self-permutation operates as a result of psychodynamic unconscious processes alleged to determine which self is appropriate for conscious awareness.

In forensic psychology, where theory and practice from the discipline of psychology are applied to legal pursuits of justice, determining truth carries high importance. Surveillance cameras can be a useful tool to help us form conclusions of intent. But what if we see and interpret those images differently? Within the adversarial process of the courtroom, psychological experts often proffer contradictory appraisals for the triers of fact to consider in their determinations of truth. Whose appraisal is correct? The answer is often the truth of the side trying its case.

Experimental research on inattentional blindness demonstrates that when information is viewed from a narrowed attentional focus, only that which is attended to is recalled. This compromised attentional focus can manifest in a self-confirmatory bias where one sees only what one is attending to, which is tantamount to a tunnel vision. America's current political climate reveals a highly polarized divide among citizens as they grapple to discern truthful discourse disseminated from the current Administration. Depending on the slant of the media outlet, we are presented with contradictory renditions and interpretations of factual events and comments made by the President and his Administration that cause bewilderment and frustration. This new type of reality, characterized as *alternative facts*, makes the determination of truth that much more complicated. Thus, while a surveillance camera might capture an image, how that image is interpreted depends on the agenda, preference, and subjective reality informing the gaze of the observer.

Gaze and Moral Action

Does mere awareness of being watched—whether externally (e.g., presence of a camera or a posted sign) or internally (e.g., overarching effects of the guilt-ridden *Superego*)—impact one's decision to behave antisocially? Social science research has investigated this question using artificial surveillance cues, such as signs depicting watching eyes, to see what impact, if any, they have on the moral nature of behavior. The results have been mixed.

Some psychological research has shown that conscious awareness of being observed alters naturally occurring behavior in a direction of being more prosocial than it would have been otherwise (Bourrat et al. 194). Specifically, researchers have found that when an image of eyes was visible prior to forming a moral judgment—on a computer screen or posted on the wall, for example—it led to lower ratings of acceptability for adverse behavioral choices. Other research has found that signs of watching eyes induce cooperative, prosocial behavior in the form of donating to charities, recycling, choosing not to litter, resisting engagement in petty crime such as stealing bicycles, and a willingness to vote (Panagopoulos and van der Linden 113). Interestingly, these researchers assert that negative emotions triggered by the signs, such as anxiety, put the brain in a heightened state of awareness that elicits a fear of punishment, which in turn leads to more prosocial actions. Moreover, the resulting prosocial acts in this study were not due to the inner voice of one's conscience, but rather to a protective mechanism against reputational threat.

Other research has demonstrated weak effects with the use of artificial surveillance cues if used alone. However, when accompanied by additional incentives, such as slogans encouraging personal investment and accountability, more prosocial behaviors were said to occur (Meleady et al. 1163; Northover et al. 570). The rationale here is that people will typically follow their regular patterns of behavior when making a decision involving behavioral regulation, but when a new behavioral standard is made salient and attention is drawn to that new standard coupled with an expressed expectation of personal agency, a different behavioral choice is more likely to ensue (Carver and Scheier 120). In the study led by Meleady, drivers were encouraged to shut off their engines rather than idling at a train crossing. Results showed that approximately 20% of motorists routinely turned their engines off without being asked. However, this amount changed to 30% when using an *instructive eyes sign* (i.e., a picture of eyes with the text: "When barriers are down switch off your engine") and to 51% when using an *instructive eyes sign* with a private self-focus (i.e., a picture of the eyes with the text: "Think of yourself: When barriers are down switch off your engine"). Thus, in contrast to previous research, it was concluded that one's perceived self-narrative (e.g., environmentally conscious, morally responsible) more so than public scrutiny was the significant factor impacting behavior in the direction of moral altruism (Meleady et al. 1167).

Contrary to prosocial behaviors, being watched has also been shown to lead to higher risk-taking behavior, as demonstrated in numerous research investigations of teen decision-making while engaged in simulated driving experiments. For example, when alone, male teens exhibited more caution when deciding whether to stop or attempt to run an amber light in the experimental condition than when being observed completing the same task by a group of friends. In the latter condition teens made more risky decisions leading to higher numbers of simulated crashes. With this particular audience, rather than being perceived as negative, being seen as a somewhat reckless, risk-taking driver was more advantageous to one's reputation.

It appears that multiple variables impact the moral decision-making process when observation in some form is involved. Whether it is fear of external sanctions in the form of criticism, punishment, or social exclusion or of internal sanctions such as an undesirable self-narrative, both sources are strong motivating forces impacting the decision-making process. What happens if one's identity is disguised? If we accept that reputational threat impacts behavioral decision-making, then obscuring one's identity should eliminate this aspect. Consider the criminal who wears a disguise to mask his appearance. This coveted action can have a twofold effect: (1) it eliminates concern for reputational threat; (2) anonymity allows the offender to create a reality where he is role-playing in costume, exercising a false self, and thus incurring less personal responsibility for his actions. This ability to disengage from personal responsibility would, in theory, increase one's ability to engage in immoral conduct. Thus, masking one's self, both literally in the case of a disguise but also figuratively in the sense of self-deception, fosters an increased potential for criminal activity.

LIMITATIONS OF SURVEILLANCE

One complication with surveillance is crime displacement. For example, while crime reduction has been noted in monitored areas such as parking lots (51%), city centers and public housing communities (70%), and public transit systems (23%), these results have been undermined by displacement effects of criminal mischief simply shifting to other unmonitored areas (Welsh and Farrington 716). A second problem concerns sustainability of morally desired behavior. When photo radar was first introduced, many drivers would be extra cautious in maintaining the posted speed limit in locations where cameras were visible. But over time this vigilance and fear of being caught seemed to dissipate and lose its effectiveness. Drivers consequently returned to their previous driving habits. Of course, one cannot assume a uniform effect for all drivers. Those particularly prone to hyper-sociality—to whom researchers Pfattheicher and Keller attribute a "chronic public self-awareness"—would likely demonstrate higher than average anxiety and thus behave in conformance with such devices, whether hooked up or not (560). Conversely, others may see such devices as an authoritarian overreach, a challenge to their personal freedom, and, consequently, drive more erratically just to be defiant.

CONCLUDING THOUGHTS

It is clear that gaze can influence moral and social conventions of behavior as it relates to some type of authentic self-presentation. It could conceivably be argued that one "is irretrievably split between his surface, front-stage behavior and his back-stage subjectivity" and as such cannot escape the *performed self* whether publicly or alone (Willis and Silbey 444). Imprisoned by both a public and imaginary audience, we remain hopelessly entwined in self-observation and appraisal as we orchestrate our self-presentation. Indeed, surveillance in its various forms facilitates a kaleidoscopic projection of selves, each with its own hopelessly biased, self-serving agenda.

When it comes to determining *truth* through the process of observation, this practice is obviously flawed. Surveillance methods, while well intentioned, possess limitations across situations and within people. Whether their purpose is to ward off criminal activity or to reveal factual evidence, both goals are compromised by the subjective influence of observer bias. We rely on media literacy to address needs for safety and a shared cultural identity. When we struggle to distinguish fact from alternative fact or truth from fabrication, we are left directionless without a compass. Unable to trust what we see, and without clear indication of how to determine authentic self-presentation, we are left ill-equipped to move forward.

WORKS CITED

Baruh, Lemi. "Publicized Intimacies on Reality Television: An Analysis of Voyeuristic Content and Its Contribution to the Appeal of Reality Programming." *Journal of*

Broadcasting & Electronic Media, vol. 53, no. 2, 2009, pp.190-210.

Berger, Allan. "The Evil Eye—An Ancient Superstition." *Journal of Religion and Health*, vol. 51, no. 4, 2012, pp. 1098-1103.

Bourrat, Pierrick, Nicolas Baumard, and Ryan McKay. "Surveillance Cues Enhance Moral Condemnation." *Evolutionary Psychology*, vol. 9, no. 2, 2011, pp. 193-19.

Carver, Charles, and Michael Scheier. "Control Theory: A Useful Conceptual Framework for Personality— Social, Clinical, and Health Psychology." *Psychological Bulletin*, vol. 92, no. 1, 1982, pp.111-135.

Christensen, Miyase, and André Jansson. "Complicit Surveillance, Interveillance, and the Question of Cosmopolitanism: Toward a Phenomenological Understanding of Mediatization." *New Media & Society*, vol. 17, no. 9, 2015, pp. 1473-1491.

Hare, Robert D. *Without Conscience: The Disturbing World of the Psychopaths Among Us.* The Guilford Press, 1993.

"Thomas Jefferson." *5 Minute Biographies.* www.5minutebiographies.com/thomas-jefferson/. Accessed 30 June 2019.

Meleady, Rose, Dominic Abrams, Julie Van de Vyver, Tim Hopthrown, Lynsey Mahmood, Abigail Player, Ruth Lamont, and Ana Leite. "Surveillance or Self-Surveillance? Behavioral Cues Can Increase the Rate of Drivers' Pro-Environmental Behavior at a Long Wait Stop." *Environmental Behavior*, vol. 49, no. 10, 2017, pp. 1156-1172.

Northover, Stefanie, William Pedersen, Adam Cohen, and Paul Andrews. "Effect of Artificial Surveillance Cues on Reported Moral Judgment: Experimental Failures to Replicate and Two Meta-Analyses." *Evolution and Human Behavior*, vol. 38, no. 5, 2016, pp. 561-571.

Orwell, George. *1984.* Harcourt Brace and Company, 1949.

Panagopoulous, Costas, and Sander van der Linden. "The Feeling of Being Watched: Do Eye Cues Elicit Negative Affect?" *North American Journal of Psychology*, vol. 19, no. 1, 2017, pp. 113-121.

Perez, Joe. "gaze." Hello Poetry, Nov. 2014, hellopoetry.com/joe-perez/. Accessed 4 April 2018.

Pfattheicher, Stefan, and Johannes Keller. "The Watching Eyes Phenomenon: The Role of a Sense of Being Seen and Public Self-Awareness." *European Journal of Social Psychology*, vol. 45, 2015, pp. 560-566.

"Surveillance." *Online Etymology Dictionary.* www.etymonline.com/word/surveillance. Accessed 30 June 2019.

Welsh, Brandon C., and David P. Farrington. "Public Area CCTV and Crime Prevention: An Updated Systematic Review and Meta-Analysis." *Justice Quarterly*, vol. 26, no. 4, 2009, pp. 716-745.

Willis, James, and Susan Silbey. "Self, Surveillance, and Society." *The Sociological Quarterly*, vol. 43, no. 3, 2002, pp. 439-445.

Withers, Christopher. "The Watcher is Watched." Hello Poetry, Sep. 2014, hellopoetry.com/poem/862357/the-watcher-is-watched/. Accessed 4 April 2018.

Surrealism as a Way of Seeing:
Zygmunt Bauman on Arts in Liquid Times

MARC VAN DEN BOSSCHE

VRIJE UNIVERSITEIT BRUSSEL
BRUSSELS, BELGIUM

ABSTRACT: *In a few places in his extensive oeuvre, the British-Polish sociologist Zygmunt Bauman (1925-2017) discusses the role of art in postmodernity and liquid modernity. His vision of art rarely receives attention from researchers. This is regrettable because in his rather pessimistic vision of the so-called liquid times, Bauman sees art as still playing a critical and liberating role.*

Bauman regards the postmodern artist's work as an almost heroic attempt to give a voice to what is ineffable and to make tangible what is invisible. In the same movement in which the artist refuses to accept the socially legitimated canon of meanings and expressions, she shows that more than one voice is possible. The artist invites us to participate in the infinite process of interpretation, which is also the process of creating meanings.

Bauman agrees with Michel Foucault that criticism is not so much a matter of showing what goes wrong, but rather of examining the seemingly obvious presuppositions we make. Art wants to question and challenge these assumptions. Bauman believes that Belgian surrealist René Magritte was in his art a precursor for this idea of Foucault. The artist experiments and takes risks but will never capture a meaning. Unlike the modernist avant-garde, the avant-garde of liquid times avoids universals and therefore any restrictive consensus on meaning. The critical role of art can be characterized as surrealistic because there is more than the given reality.

KEYWORDS: liquid modernity, aesthetics, art and politics, Zygmunt Bauman, surrealism

A liquid life is one that is lived in conditions of constant uncertainty. This life takes place in a society that the Polish-British sociologist and philosopher Zygmunt Bauman (1925-2017) has coined *liquid modernity*. The circumstances of people's lives change so fast in such a society that they never have the chance to acquire any solidity or to become habitual and routine. Moreover, a liquid life is one that is completely focused on consumption. Practically everything in our environment, whether material or spiritual, can serve as an object of consumption. And, Bauman contends, we also treat ourselves as such: the liquid life feeds itself with a constant gnawing feeling of inadequacy and dissatisfaction about and with the self.

This somewhat unsettling assertion summarizes the core idea of Bauman's book *Liquid Life*. One in a series of works whose titles start with *liquid*, these publications deal with love, fear, evil and the times in which we live. The tone for the entire series was set by *Liquid Modernity*, published at the start of the second millennium, in which Bauman wanted to shift the focus of his interpretation of these times. What he originally called postmodern is now termed *liquid modern*. A glance at the titles of a few of the other works in Bauman's qualitatively and quantitatively impressive *oeuvre* makes it seem that the man is not the most cheerful of messengers. The ominous titles include *Wasted Lives*, *Moral Blindness*, *Collateral Damage* and *State of Crisis*. I doubt that anyone picks them up because they look like pleasant reading, but like any story, Bauman's work can be read in an alternative way. Here, I will endeavor to show the positive force behind the gloomy covers. Bauman's critique is not in fact fatalistic; instead, it can be seen as a powerful appeal. Bauman tells us that the way we live is just one of several possibilities.

MODERNITY: THE PURSUIT OF CERTAINTY

Zygmunt Bauman does not perceive modernity as a historical phase that has since drawn to a close. It is rather a project and, as we will see further on, one that continues within what is known as post- and liquid modernity. However, the big difference between the latter two philosophies and the original project of modernity is encapsulated in the hope, or rather, the illusion, that goes with it. In Bauman's view, modernity is a plan for expelling ambivalence and uncertainty. The hope or illusion was that this project would one day reach completion. It is this illusion that has been abandoned.

It is easy to believe that people consider the overcoming of ambivalence and uncertainty as something desirable and even necessary. Humans prefer stability in life and therefore like to cling to the ideals that offer the prospect of certainty. Just think about the question of identity that characterizes current debates. Many prefer not to see identity—which derives from *identitas*, something that stays the same, as flexible or fluid. By extension, the term *ambivalence* has an almost entirely negative connotation. But Bauman has a radically different view of this. After all, the crusade for the expulsion of ambivalence is invariably accompanied by exclusion and dominance. We want to either exclude what is different or dominate it, which is to say, model it on ourselves.

In fact, Bauman has little or nothing good to say about what he calls modernity. To him, it is a plan for control, rational rule (over nature, for example), planning and steering. Technocracy and bureaucracy are obvious forms of this. Modernity is practically obsessive about order, clarity, and restraint. It allows for zero ambivalence: A is A and under no circumstances B. In *Modernity and Ambivalence*, describes it in following terms:

> An orderly world is a world in which 'one knows how to go on' (or, what amounts to the same, one knows how to find out—and find out *for sure*—how to go on), in which one knows how to calculate the probability of an event and how to increase and decrease that probability; a world in which links between certain situations, and the effectivity of certain actions remain by

and large constant, so that one can rely on past successes as guides for future ones. (1-2)

The modern world strives for a rational order that pretends to be universal. This way of thinking, driven by science and technology, would need to spread across the world. After all, this singular model stands for a truth that should be universally accepted. Bauman believes, therefore, that this endeavor, characteristic of Western culture, is inseparable from a plan for the domination of other cultures and for inclusion and exclusion. Bauman is caustic in his observations: "Intolerance is, therefore, the natural inclination of modern practice" (*Modernity and Ambivalence* 8).

Later in *Modernity and Ambivalence*, he remarks that there are friends and enemies, and then there are strangers. Friends and enemies actually have equal status. One is the opposite of the other, but their standing is clear. Friendship and enmity have always been party to how we shape society. A more pleasant way to think of this is to consider the difference between political allies and political opponents. A well-functioning democracy should be able to handle these differences in a sensible way. This is not the case when it comes to foreigners. Within the modernist scheme, they are neither friend nor foe. The stranger evades this modern antagonism of (democratic) opponents and thereby threatens to undermine the very foundations of society. He or she is neither friend nor enemy and may be either. But we do not know and we do not know how we can know. The foreigner is *undecidable* and escapes the usual bifurcation of ally and opponent. This means, for example, that strangers, such as asylum seekers or refugees, are denied political rights. Consider all the current noise about how efficiently we can exclude or deport them.

Bauman's most celebrated book, *Modernity and the Holocaust*, focuses sharply on this modernist kind of thinking. In his opinion, the Holocaust—the organization of the deportation and genocide of the Jewish people by the Nazis—was only made possible through the tools supplied by modernist thinking. Without an efficiently organized bureaucracy, the Holocaust could never have been implemented in the way we now know it was. The Holocaust is the epitome of excluding people and turning them into strangers—of dehumanizing them. Bauman is speaking here from his own experiences as a Jew, but even more so from his wife Janina's experiences in the Warsaw ghetto. It is worth reading her *Winter in the Morning*.

POSTMODERNITY: LIFE IN FRAGMENTS

Postmodernity is the modernity that comes to terms with its own impossibility. In *Postmodern Ethics*, Bauman asserts that postmodernity is modernity without the illusions. We know what these illusions are from the previous paragraph. Modernity wanted order and clarity and did not shy away from methods that led to exclusion and domination. Instructed by Bauman's "Strangers: The Social Construction of Universality and Particularity," we can speak of *making* strangers. Strangeness is a social construct.

So, what does it mean that postmodernity has given up modernist illusions? In three books in which Bauman describes the phenomenon of postmodernity, his thinking takes a positive, even optimistic, turn. These three books are titled *Intimations of Postmodernity*, *Postmodern Ethics,* and *Life in Fragments*. They were published between 1992 and 1995. Two years later, they were followed by a work with a less hopeful title, *Postmodernity and Its Discontents.*

If we see postmodernity as a project too, then this would be described as 'learning to live with the quiet chaos of uncertainty.' We suddenly seemed to realize that all systems are contingent, that is to say not necessary but also not impossible, and that applies equally to alternative systems. In that sense, postmodernity accepts that there will never be an order obtained that is unambiguous and uniform and that there will always be a plurality of human worldviews. And the postmodern individual is able to accept that.

In *Postmodern Ethics*, Bauman makes the emboldened statement that the postmodern person has learned to respect ambiguity again. We can even give legitimacy to that which we may not understand and that may even fall outside our own paradigms. The world does not suddenly become a better place, but at least the postmodern persons realize that they may have to approach the situation as it is and deal with all its actual hurdles. The *other* may be radically different and alien to our worldview but we can reconcile this with a form of morality that acknowledges and respects this difference. Postmodern ethics seeks to be inclusive (*Postmodern Ethics* 31-36).

In *Intimations of Postmodernity*, Bauman calls postmodernity *a state of mind* (vii). In essence, it is a life without truth. For Bauman, this life without truth is a life that has said goodbye to the modernist quest for certainty, order, and homogeneity. And that means also parting with a truth that would be universally valid. This means, for example, that the idea of Western culture involved not only a quest for world power but also a mission that assumed its own moral superiority. Bauman would go on to describe this in later texts as moral blindness or as *unmoralization* caused by only approaching the other in terms of an instrumental, technical mindset in which ethical rules are claimed to be universal despite the particularity of circumstances and of people.

Bauman does see that this involves a paradox. On the one hand, postmodernism seeks to give individuals a greater moral sensibility and make them morally responsible for the *other* who does not fit into our categories of thinking. But on the other hand, these individuals then find themselves in the dark: since there are no longer any ethical criteria considered to be universal, they fall into a sort of moral desolation. Bauman admits that it is not easy to find the golden mean between modernistic colonization of others and potential indifference. He relies on increased solidarity between postmodern individuals. Whereas the modernist bias led to exclusion and inhumanity, Bauman hopes that people will once again experience a form of morality that is distinct from established ethical principles and which precedes them. People would then be open to what Bauman, with reference to the French philosopher Emmanuel Levinas, calls "the Other as [the] Face." (*Postmodern Ethics* 48, 74). Bauman believes that moral duty, regarded as a universal rule, makes people uniform. The morality that he wishes to replace it with is not one that he sees as a rule to be followed, but as a non-rational and non-computable capability of being morally addressed by the other. We are moral before we even think and before society has imposed moral rules on us. So, for example, instead of perceiving refugees as an economic—and therefore calculable—problem, we would see them fully as individuals who are making a moral appeal to us. To repeat: inclusion and exclusion is at the forefront of what Bauman describes as postmodernity. In *Life in Fragments*, Bauman states explicitly that this is the point where the choice between good and evil begins (2).

Liquid Modernity: The Certainty of Uncertainty

The moment that Bauman adjusts his terminology and no longer speaks of postmodernity but of liquid modernity, his hopeful tone about unconditional morality and the increased moral sensibility associated with it also changes. In *Liquid Modernity*, he writes about his strong conviction that change is the only permanence and uncertainty the only certainty left. Liquid times demand a constant pursuit of improvement and renewal but they have no ultimate goal in mind. Society will never reach the point where society-as-a-project is completed. Moreover, Bauman asks whether society has not become convinced that Margaret Thatcher was correct when she made her famous *TINA* statement: "There Is No Alternative."

A memorable, if not very flattering, image that Bauman uses to characterize the state of affairs in liquid modern times is that of a mobile home park. If the neighbors do not turn up their TVs too loud and leave us in peace, no one will raise a critical voice. If they do make too much noise, then we turn to the hoped-for authority of the manager. And this authority is not in itself questioned (*Liquid Modernity* 23-25).

This analogy allows us to understand why Bauman puts two phenomena at the heart of his reflections on liquid modernity: that of individualization and that of excessive consumerism. Bauman sees individualization as a problem. In fact, we can no longer escape it. We are constantly addressed as individuals and held responsible as such. Social problems have suddenly become individual problems. Are you ill or unemployed? That is your problem and not that of society. Furthermore, our individuality only becomes manifest in our lives as consumers. Everything has become volatile and options appear to be infinite. We shop an identity for ourselves. Bauman fears that if our identities are created by consumption, then we are ultimately in competition with each other and that inhibits cooperation and solidarity. In *Liquid Life*, Bauman says that this consumerism is an economy of dissatisfaction, excess, and waste. However, contrary to what we would imagine, these are not negative characteristics but precisely a sign of health from the perspective of consumer society. In fact, the three traits ensure that liquid society continually renews itself and keeps running on its chosen path—that is to say on a path that no longer has a destination, unless it is more consumption and innovation for innovation's sake.

ENCOUNTERS IN A LIQUID CITY

As mentioned above, Bauman's analysis is not optimistic. But perhaps he just wants to open our eyes to how we experience the freedom that abandoning the hierarchical, ordered, end-goal-oriented modernist model has given us. Since everything is fluid and uncertain, this actually means that there is an alternative. *TINA* is not true. *TINA* does not make sense. Believing in *TINA* is self-affirming and nothing more.

In his lesser-known work *Culture in a Liquid Modern World*, Bauman refers approvingly to a text about the legacy of Europe by the German philosopher Hans-Georg Gadamer. In it, Gadamer states that living with others, and living as the other of others, is quintessential to being human and that this can occur in the most exalted manner as well as the most unpleasant. Gadamer perceives the great opportunity of Europe: the chance and the duty to learn the art of living with others. We may have great differences in the ways that we shape our lives and give them meaning, but we still share the same purview, notably that of a democratic society that respects plurality and diversity. Differences merge in what Gadamer calls a *fusion of horizons* (*Culture in a Liquid Modern World* 85-6). We respect differences but we also see what we have in common and how we can build a diverse, democratic and inclusive society from this commonality. However, in order to see this common ground, we need contact and dialogue. Bauman takes this idea further and writes that a culture should ensure that artists come into contact with their audience. Art events in the city are a perfect means to make this happen. Art meets the public and therefore puts it in contact with diverse forms of expression. Plurality and diversity are given room for mutual exchanges. In *Babel*, a dialogue between Bauman and Ezio Mauro, Bauman claims that the city is now the destination and that we can give our creativity free rein there to strengthen our communality and be strong citizens. Urban life will always remain ambivalent and comprehend both *mixophilia* and *mixophobia*, both the love and fear of living with others. In *Liquid Times*, Bauman refers to the role preserved for architects. When shared spaces are created then there is also space for the fusion of horizons. Cities can be laboratories for ways to handle differences. Art can portray the differences. In a book about the necessity of sociology, Bauman, inspired by Milan Kundera, claims that it is the task of both art and sociology to let people tear through the canvas of prejudice (*Liquid Modernity* 202-3).

LIQUID ARTS

In "Liquid Arts," an article that explicitly refers in its title to the fluidity of art, Zygmunt Bauman asks us to imagine every society as a large room containing a multitude of furniture, wallpaper, prints on walls, corners and hooks of all kinds, and dark spots. Many doors lead to this room. Next to each door is an electrical switch which in all cases gives a different color in terms of light in the room. Bauman points out what photographers know very well: each different color filter gives a different end result. Some elements that remained in the shade suddenly appear to come out clearly when using another filter and vice versa. And then, of course, the intention is that at each visit we use a different door to enter the room and therefore also a different switch that gives different light and makes us see things in the room differently. In this article, Bauman wants to use the image of the door of art to comment about modern liquid society.

For Bauman, art can no longer play the role of the former—modernist—avant-garde: it is no longer possible to show one way to the true destination. The meaning of post-modern art and art in liquid modernity is now about showing multiple paths. In *Postmodernity and Its Discontents,* Bauman observes: "In my opinion, the meaning of post-modern art is to open the door widely to many forms of meaning" (111). With this vision, Bauman joins the role that Michel Foucault saw for criticism. Criticism for Foucault is no longer a matter of saying which things are wrong as they are. Rather, as this last quotation shows, Bauman is concerned with the ways in which meaning is created. The critical attitude seeks out the assumptions, which unquestioned and unchallenged as ways of thinking are underlying practices that we consider to be evident.

Bauman refers to the Belgian surrealist René Magritte as the forerunner of this idea by Foucault. The artist experiments and takes risks, but never records a meaning. Unlike the modernist avant-garde, in liquid times the avant-garde will avoid any possibility of a future universal and thus restrictive consensus on meaning. This way, the critical role of art is surrealistic: there is more to it than the given reality. Criticism is about making easy gestures difficult. Bauman can bring this vision seamlessly into line with a statement he quotes from Magritte: "This visual experience, which questions the real world, allows me to believe in the infinite possibilities of life that are still unknown. I know that I am not the only one who sees this search as the only purpose and only valid reason for human existence" (*Postmodernity and Its Discontents* 111).

Bauman's attitude towards the self-introduced understanding of the fluidity of our lives and the times in which those lives are shaped and given shape, carries with it a certain ambivalence. The problem with the liquidity of our consumer culture is undoubtedly that it threatens to divide the world into two spheres: those who can take part in the consumer game and those who cannot. It is also about our dealings with the stranger within and outside our own culture and, in general, with what Bauman has called wasted lives.

But what could be the positive side of the story of a liquefied existence? More specifically, how can the abovementioned quotation by the surrealist Magritte and the obvious positive drive that goes with it be linked to the contemporary state of art, which has itself become fluid? My answer to this should sound positive: the door of art can be used to show that the world is ambiguous, that the world can be different, that we can learn to live with a multiplicity of ways of giving meaning.

WORKS CITED

Bauman, Zygmunt. "Strangers: The Social Construction of Universality and Particularity." *Telos*, vol. 78, 1988, pp. 7-42.

---. "Liquid Arts." *Theory, Culture & Society*, vol. 24, no. 1, 2007b, pp. 117-26.

---. *Collateral Damage: Social Inequalities in a Global Age*. Polity Press, 2011.

---. *Consuming Life*. Polity Press, 2007a.

---. *Culture in a Liquid Modern World*. Polity Press, 2011.

---. *Intimations of Postmodernity*. Routledge, 1992.

---. *Life in Fragments: Essays in Postmodern Morality*. Blackwell, 1995.

---. *Liquid Fear*. Polity Press, 2006.

---. *Liquid Life*. Polity Press, 2005.

---. *Liquid Love*. Polity Press, 2003.

---. *Liquid Modernity*. Polity Press, 2012/2000.

---. *Modernity and Ambivalence*. Polity Press, 1991.

---. *Modernity and the Holocaust*. Polity Press, 1989.

---. *Postmodern Ethics*. Blackwell, 1993.

---. *Postmodernity and Its Discontents*. Polity Press, 1997.

---. *The Art of Life*. Polity Press, 2008.

---. *The Individualized Society*. Polity Press, 2001.

---. *Vloeibare tijden. Leven in een eeuw van onzekerheid*. Zoetermeer: Klement, 2011.

---. *Wasted Lives: Modernity and its Outcasts*. Polity Press, 2004.

Bauman, Zygmunt, and Carlo Bordoni. *State of Crisis*. Polity Press, 2014.

Bauman, Zygmunt, and Ezio Mauro. *Babel*. Polity Press, 2016.

Bauman, Zygmunt, and Leonidas Donskis. *Moral Blindness: The Loss of Sensitivity in Liquid Modernity*. Polity Press, 2013.

Foucault, Michel. *Politics, Philosophy, Culture: Interviews and Other Writings 1977-1984*. Routledge, 1988.

The Algo-Artist

Galit Wellner

The NB School of Design
Haifa, Israel
and
Tel Aviv University
Tel Aviv, Israel

ABSTRACT: *Imagination has been praised as a basic human capability. For Kant, it is what enables perception and understanding. For Marx, it is unique to humans and a characteristic of human labor that makes it distinct from that of animals like bees or spiders. In the age when technologies replaced human muscles, imagination could have been considered exclusively human. But in the digital age, when algorithms start replacing human thinking, the faculty of imagination should be reexamined.*

The question is whether the actions of AI algorithms can be regarded as imagination. This article focuses on the ways in which algorithmic imagination functions. To assess whether algorithms can imagine, we first need to ask what imagination is. The first part of the article provides a brief overview of the classical modern answer to imagination as provided by Immanuel Kant. This part ends with a provocative demonstration of how present-day algorithms follow Kant's description of human imagination. If algorithms perform imagination that has been conceived as unique to humans, then a new form of imagination should be sought. The second part of the article offers an alternative model of imagination that may fit the contemporary mode of operation of the imagination where humans and AI interact and co-shape each other through media technologies.

KEYWORDS: imagination, artificial intelligence, co-shaping, Kant, layers

Introduction

In 1968, Philip K. Dick published his well-known novel *Do Androids Dream of Electric Sheep?* Fifty years later we still ask the same question but with different wording. We switch from androids to algorithms and ask, "Can algorithms imagine electric sheep?" Today this is not a theoretical question, as some artificial intelligence (AI) algorithms already attempt to imagine and even create art. Take for example Google's Project Magenta that was formed to meet challenges like: "Can we use machine learning to create compelling art and music? If so, how? If not, why not?"[1] One of the tools developed as part of this project is SketchRNN in which the algorithm learns how to draw a figure like a cat. Once the algorithm is trained, it takes any doodle the user scribbles and turns it into a simple drawing of a cat. Each time the algorithm operates, a new form of cat is created. The more interesting option is the ability to create hybrids, like combing a cat with

---

[1] See "Make Music and Art Using Machine Learning." *Magenta,* magenta.tensorflow.org/.

a truck or a chair. The algorithm produces many imaginative permutations of a cat-chair or cat-truck (Ha and Eck 8). Can we consider this functionality as imagination? Is imagination unique to humans?

If imagination is not unique to humans and can be imputed also to algorithms, does it mean that technologies can create art? On the one hand, algorithms can be regarded as mere tools, like brushes for the painter and cameras for the photographer. On the other, algorithms operate on a different logic. Unlike tools (like a brush) and machines (like a camera), these digital technologies can replace the artist. While machines of the first industrial revolution replaced workers' muscles, algorithms of what Norbert Wiener terms as the second industrial revolution target human mental capabilities (27). Digital technologies have been making mathematic calculations much faster than most human beings, but this is nothing new. What is new today is the ways in which AI tries to imagine starting with recommendation engines that attempt to predict which song the user might like or what the user might mean when typing "apple"—the fruit or the company? What is the destination when the user starts typing "aku"—is it Akureyri or a typo? Some algorithms try to imagine with no input from a specific user. They compose pop songs, improvise jazz sessions, or draw artistic pictures.[2]

The question is whether their actions can be regarded as imagination. This article focuses on the ways in which what I term here "algorithmic imagination" functions. To assess if algorithms can imagine we first need to ask what imagination is. The first part of the article provides a brief overview of the classical modern answer to imagination as provided by Immanuel Kant. This part ends with a provocative demonstration of how present-day algorithms follow Kant's description of human imagination. If algorithms perform imagination that has been conceived as unique to humans, then a new form of imagination should be sought. The second part of the article offers an alternative model of imagination that may fit the contemporary mode of operation of the imagination where humans and AI interact and co-shape each other through media technologies.

WHAT IS IMAGINATION?

Imagination has been praised as a basic human capability. In *Capital*, Karl Marx identifies imagination along with labor as unique for humans. He writes:

> a bee puts to shame many architects in the construction of her cells. But what distinguishes the worst architect from the best of bees is this, that the architect raises the structure *in imagination*

---

[2] For Sony's algorithms that composed a pop song named "Daddy's Car," see the works cited for an article by Chris Mench. For improvising jazz, see the *Shimon Robot and Friends* website for the Shimon robot created by Gil Weinberg at Georgia Institute of Technology. For drawing pictures, see the Painting Fool developed by Simon Colton at the Computational Creativity Research Group, Goldsmiths College, London.

before he erects it in reality. (83, emphasis added)

For Marx, imagination does not exist in animals like bees. It is the distinctive characteristic of human labor.[3] Marx's concept of imagination can relate back to Kant's transcendental and productive imagination as defined in his Critiques.

In *Critique of Pure Reason*, Kant terms transcendental imagination as that which enables the synthesis between perception, sensations, and intuitions on the one hand and understanding on the other. Imagination combines them into cognition in a double step: it synthesizes the manifold of intuition and performs on that manifold a "schematism" of concepts. Kant stresses that "the schema is clearly distinguishable from the image" (121) and "cannot be reduced into any image" (122). The schema functions "as a rule for the determination of our intuition, in conformity with a certain general conception" (122). In other words, the schema is like a common denominator for a certain group of images. With the concept of the schema, imagination bridges between perception and understanding thereby serving as the foundation of all knowledge and experience of the world. For example, when a manifold is synthesized in accordance with the concepts *yellow* and *circle*, the outcome can be the figure of a smiley. Thus, imagination is an a priori function that unites knowledge with sensation, passivity and activity.[4] The transcendental imagination appeared in the first edition of *Critique of Pure Reason* (1781) and was omitted six years later in the second edition (1787). In his *Kant and the Problem of Metaphysics*, Heidegger interprets the transcendental imagination as a "pure aspect" that "consists in bringing into view" (138). It is not an intermediary faculty but a primary and indispensable precondition of all knowledge. According to this interpretation, imagination combines various points of view (the "manifold" in Kant's terminology) according to the "schemata."[5]

In *Critique of the Power of Judgement* (1790), Kant "frees" imagination from understanding and regards the "free play" between them as the "productive imagination." It is a basic feature of aesthetics and art for art viewers and artists alike since it produces combinations of perceptions.[6] It can be regarded a reflection on the sensory input without determining what the object is. In the artistic context, yellow and circle may yield additional options like a sunflower or a sun. Kearney exemplifies the Kantian notion of imagination in the artistic context via Van Gogh's famous painting of *A Pair of Shoes*:

---

[3] Imagination for Marx is distinctive both in the age of the tool and the age of the machine. He refers to imagination to distinguish between human and animal activities in order to explain that not only machines are unique to humans but also tools. If animals have tools, according to this logic, then ancient humanity that did not yet have machines might lose its alleged superiority. In the digital age, when algorithms start replacing human thinking, the faculty of imagination can be imputed not only to animals but also to technologies. See Wellner's "Posthuman Imagination: From Modernity to Augmented Reality" 45-46.

[4] See also Romele 99.

[5] See also Kearney 190 and Matherne 59.

[6] See Kneller 3, Kearney 156, Matherne 62.

In ordinary experience . . . we recognize an object—say a pair of shoes—by first forming an image of an object like the one we are now applying to the relevant concept (i.e. of shoeness). We can only apprehend this object in front of us as a pair of shoes because we can form other images of other pairs of shoes. It is when the pair of shoes ceases to be perceived in the real world and becomes instead an imaginary object of art—as in Van Gogh's painting of the peasant shoes—that we experience aesthetic pleasure. Now the imagination is free to work with itself alone. It is no longer bound to any external reference. Its end is exclusively internal, autonomous. (Kearney 173)

Interestingly, this recipe for artistic imagination is now deployed in AI algorithms: Google's SketchRNN follows these guidelines when its algorithm takes the concept of "shoeness" or "catness" and projects it on a doodle drawn by the user. The software complements the doodle according to the selected theme, each time producing through "a free play" different drawings of the themed figure. The role of human imagination changes. Within this framework, it can express itself in the conceptualization of new combinations like cat-chair.

TOWARDS AN ALTERNATIVE APPROACH TO IMAGINATION

Regarding imagination as a fixed faculty across generations leads us to the conclusion that algorithms exercise imagination although it is unique to humans. An alternative view of imagination may provide a solution. It is a view that regards imagination genealogically as a faculty that changes over time. Richard Kearney maps three main paradigms of imagination in the artistic context that comprise three genealogical steps: "the *mimetic* paradigm of the premodern (i.e. biblical, classical and medieval) imagination; the *productive* paradigm of the modern imagination; and the *parodic* paradigm of the postmodern imagination" (17). According to the mimetic paradigm, the ancient artist was no more than "a craftsman who, at best, models his activity on the 'original' activity of a Divine Creator" (12). From early modernity on, the paradigm has been that of an inventor who is not bound to god, nature, and the like but is rather free to use his imagination. It is probably termed "productive" after Kant's third *Critique*. In postmodernity the "artist-inventor" is replaced by the "*bricoleur*: someone who plays around with fragments of meaning which he himself has not created" (13).

Each paradigm has its own metaphor: the mirror, the lamp, and the labyrinth of looking-glasses. The metaphors demonstrate the different mode-of-operation of each paradigm. For example, the modern lamp enlightens one facet of an object, so that under the modern regime being imaginative means to creatively shed a new light on a yet-unknown aspect. The postmodern imagination is as confusing as a labyrinth of looking glasses and leads to nowhere. For Kearney this last stage is a "threat to abolish the humanist imagination"

(13) and so contemporary imagination is "like all species under threat of extinction" (6). Kearney is not optimistic about the future of the postmodern imagination: "The concept of imagination cannot, apparently, survive the postmodern age of deconstruction. It is slowly being erased, to adapt Foucault's vivid phrase, like a face drawn in sand at the edge of the sea" (30).[7]

Kearney points to a dead-end in imagination. But what if he witnesses imagination in a transition period, where one form evaporates while the new one is not in place yet? In the next section, a new phase will be presented. It is positioned after Kearney's mimetic and productive paradigms.

From Modern Imagination to Digital Imagination

Against Kearney, I argue that imagination has not disappeared but rather has transformed. What has disappeared is the mode of operation of modern imagination that seeks new perspectives. If one looks for the good old modern form, then the inevitable conclusion is that of extinction. This conclusion can be avoided if we regard human imagination not as a stable faculty operating the same way across generations, but rather as a reflection of a dynamic technological environment and constantly changing cultural values. Assuming that every age is characterized by a new way of producing new ideas and new images, imagination today seems to be dramatically different from that of the modern era (Wellner, *Posthuman Imagination* 61).

It has already been noticed that the capitalistic culture has a huge impact on imagination as Stiegler's reading of Adorno and Horkheimer shows. But capitalism is not the only change agent. Imagination has transformed also because of the technologies that surround us. In the complex co-shaping process between humans and technologies, both sides transform (Verbeek 12). Media technologies can serve as a good example for this co-shaping.

In the 20th century, modern imagination was co-shaped by media technologies, namely photography, cinema, and television. Such an imagination focused on finding a new point of view. These media technologies showed us scenes that occur in remote locations like other continents, battlefields, or the Earth from space. Sometimes they simply revealed the familiar from a fresh new perspective like a corner of a well-known street, famous people in a private moment, or someone's expressive face. All these conform to Kearney's lamp metaphor that sheds a new light on a given aspect.

Whereas modern imagination is a faculty that produces new points of view as defined by Kant, contemporary imagination has a different logic. I designate the 21st century's imagination as "digital" and situate it in a digitally saturated environment, where digital technologies mediate ever-increasing portions of the world. Reality becomes technologically intensive so

---

[7] Kearney's pessimistic outlook can be attributed to the common criticism that today's imagination is shaped by television and advertisements led by thinkers like Bernard Stiegler in *Technics and Time, 2: Disorientation* 70.

that even communication between people is mediated more by digital technologies and performed less as a face-to-face interaction. Imagination is no exception and it is frequently enabled and managed by digital technologies. This is what Alberto Romele terms "*e*magination" (104). The term designates the ability of digital technologies to participate in the Kantian schematization as well as to reconfigure some parts of the human imagination.

What is the role of human imagination in this scenario? How does it function in a digital environment? To explain how digital technologies facilitate imagination, I propose the layer paradigm. Digital technologies operate by layering information on top of a basic layer, which is often a representation of the real world. The layers' information can be fictive (like Pokémons) or real (like products' prices, food's nutritional values, or people's names). The layers can come in any order and they lack any hierarchy. In the technology realm, this paradigm is known as augmented reality (Manovich, *The Poetics of Augmented Space* 223; Wellner, *Postphenomenological Inquiry* 61-76). AI adds autonomy and intentionality to the layers so that they can guide the user's imagination.

Interestingly, today's algorithmic imagination is mostly based on a technology known as neural networking. Inspired by the brain's neuronal structures, the algorithm builds layers of processes. Each layer-process deals with a fragment of the total task. For example, one layer translates visible dots into lines so that the next level can decipher a group of lines and detect from it a figure. A third layer identifies the color of the figure. Another example is Google's DeepDream Generator whose algorithm receives a picture as its baseline and develops it into a hallucinatory image. In each stage-layer, the picture is tweaked and modified in the selected direction. The result is frequently dreamy and artistic.

It is important to note that the resemblance of the human and the digital neuronal mechanisms does not mean that one imitates the other. The concept of co-shaping rejects statements like "software imitates with increasing fidelity the way human productive imagination works" or "in the age of big data, the digital imagination is going to have the upper hand on human imagination" (Romele 107, 113). Rather, it means they come close to each other and, in that process, one complements or extends the other. Both the human and the digital keep changing continuously. Moreover, the layered model as well as the co-shaping concept refrain from positioning one imagination as superior to the other.

The layered structure resembles Deleuze and Guattari's model of plateaus.[8] To explain what a plateau is, Deleuze and Guattari describe how they wrote their book *A Thousand Plateaus*:

---

[8] They attribute the origin of the term to Gregory Bateson who designated the word 'plateau' to "a continuous, self-vibrating region of intensities whose development avoids any orientation toward a culmination point or external end" (Deleuze and Guattari 1-2).

Each morning we would wake up, and each of us would ask himself what plateau he was going to tackle, writing five lines here, ten there. We had hallucinatory experiences, we watched lines leave one plateau and proceed to another like columns of tiny ants. We made circles of convergence. Each plateau can be read starting anywhere and can be related to any other plateau. (22)

This form of creative writing progresses in several directions simultaneously and rejects the traditional linear-hierarchical movement. Augmented reality's layers operate like plateaus. Thus, they direct the user's imagination towards a new mode of operation, no less creative and free. The role of human imagination in augmented reality is to create new layers and identify links between existing layers. AI can provide contents for the layers but can hardly suggest new ones or novel combinations of them. This mode of operation, I argue, is dramatically different from that of the modern imagination. The viewer becomes a user who not only views from various perspectives but can also creatively establish new layers or link existing layers into innovative combinations. If for Kant imagination is the synthesis of sensation and understanding (106), then in the digital era the interrogation should seek to model the role of technology in sensation and understanding.

IMAGINATION AND ART

In his book *The Wake of Imagination*, Kearney shows that the link between art and imagination has a long history. He correctly assumes that being an artist requires a certain amount of imagination, and that imagination is something that everyone has, thereby following Kant's statement that each and every person is a potential artist. But being an artist involves certain technologies. This is where postphenomenology becomes crucial for the analysis. This theory and its methodology direct us to examine the technologies involved and the relations between them and the users-artists. In ancient times, painting required coloring materials. In modernity, it was a camera. Today, we should ask what it means to be an artist if one replaces the coloring material and cameras with software code and screens? A cue can be found in DeepDream's opening screen that states: "human AI collaboration."[9] Algorithmic art might mean a new division of work between algorithms and users: the algorithmic imagination contributes by generating contents for the various layers and offering new combinations; the users operate their imagination by thinking of new layers and by generating meaning to the combinations found by the algorithms. Thus, the technological imagination remains somewhat bounded to the modernist sense of generating new perspectives with each layer, leaving to the human imagination the tasks of establishing new layers and finding meaning in unexpected combinations.

---

[9] See "Human AI Collaboration." *Deep Dream Generator*, 2019, deepdreamgenerator.com/. Accessed 30 May 2019.

AI algorithms can be positioned as tools for human artists for the creation of new contents. The software provides what Don Ihde terms "micro perceptions" and defines as the "immediate and focused bodily [impression] in actual seeing, hearing etc." (29). A micro-perception is sensory by its nature. Many contemporary digital technologies already mechanize micro-perceptions. Siri, Alexa, and security cameras are some examples of technologies that produce micro-perceptions independently of their human users. But algorithms can hardly provide the macro-perception that is "the hermeneutic-cultural signifying dimension of a situated experience" (Ihde 29). The algorithmic macro-perception is frequently no more than a statistical aggregation of existing data (Manovich, "Automating Aesthetics" 6). For example, what does it mean that a certain zip code is associated with a higher risk of not returning a loan? We need the human user to assign meaning to this combination and explain that poor neighborhoods are indeed riskier, but this parameter should be morally rejected. Otherwise, those who live in poor areas are punished by a higher interest rate. It becomes a self-fulfilling prophecy. The "macro perceptions" in their deep sense can be performed only by the human artist-operator. This division of labor keeps the human in the picture and redefines what it means to be an artist and what imagination is in the 21st century.

WORKS CITED

Deleuze, Gilles, and Felix Guattari. *A Thousand Plateaus: Capitalism and Schizophrenia*. Translated by Brian Massumi. University of Minnesota Press, 1987.

Ha, David, and Douglas Eck. "A Neural Representation of Sketch Drawings." *arXiv*, 1704.03477, 19 May 2017, arxiv.org/pdf/1704.03477.pdf.

Heidegger, Martin. *Kant and the Problem of Metaphysics*. Indiana University Press, 1968.

Ihde, Don. *Technology and the Lifeworld: From Garden to Earth*. Indiana University Press, 1990.

Kearney, Richard. *The Wake of Imagination*. Routledge, 1988.

Kneller, Jane. *Kant and the Power of Imagination*. Cambridge University Press, 2007.

Manovich, Lev. "Automating Aesthetics: Artificial Intelligence and Image Culture." *manovich*, 2017, manovich.net/content/04-projects/101-automating-aesthetics-artificial-intelligence-and-image-culture/automating_aesthetics.pdf. Accessed 4 March 2018.

---. "The Poetics of Augmented Space." *Visual Communications*, vol. 5, no. 2, 2006, pp. 219-240.

Marx, Karl. *Capital: A Critique of Political Economy*. Pacific Publishing Studio, 2010.

Matherne, Samantha. "Kant's Theory of the Imagination." *The Routledge Handbook of Philosophy of Imagination*, edited by Amy Kind, Routledge, 2016, pp. 75-88.

Mench, Chris. "It Happened: 'Daddy's Car' Is a Song Created by Artificial Intelligence." *Complex*, 22 September 2016, www.complex.com/music/2016/09/artificial-intelligence-new-song-daddys-car.

Romele, Alberto. "Imaginative Machines." *Techné: Research in Philosophy and Technology*, vol. 22, no. 1, 2018, pp. 98-125.

Shimon Robot and Friends. www.shimonrobot.com/video. Accessed 30 May 2019.

Stiegler, Bernard. *Technics and Time, 2: Disorientation*. Translated by Stephen Barker. Stanford University Press, 2009.

The Painting Fool, 2000-2019, www.thepaintingfool.com/index.html. Accessed 30 May 2019.

Verbeek, Peter-Paul. *What Things Do: Philosophical Reflections on Technology, Agency, and Design*. The Pennsylvania State University Press, 2005.

Wellner, Galit. *A Postphenomenological Inquiry of Cell Phones: Genealogies, Meanings, and Becoming*. Lexington Books, 2016.

---. "Posthuman Imagination: From Modernity to Augmented Reality." Journal of Posthuman Studies, vol. 2, no. 1, 2018, pp. 45-66.

Contributors

BAS DE BOER is a Ph.D. candidate in philosophy of technology at the University of Twente in the Netherlands. He is writing a dissertation on how imaging technologies in the (cognitive) neurosciences mediate scientific knowledge of human behavior. His research interests are in philosophy of technology, (post-)phenomenology, and French epistemology.

ADRIANA DURÁN GUERRERO is full time Associate C Research Professor at Benemérita Universidad Autónoma de Puebla, Escuela de Artes Plásticas y Audiovisuales and serves as the Coordinator for the School of Cinematography. Her research and praxis focus on nonfiction film, narrative discourse, and the visual as a way of seeing and explaining ourselves to the world. She teaches Cinematographic Language, Nonfiction Film, and Theory of Moving Images.

ALEJANDRA DE LAS MERCEDES FERNÁNDEZ teaches courses in Political Philosophy and Aesthetics. She participates in a Research Project focusing on transdisciplinary approaches to corporeality in politics and art.

LUANNE FRANK holds a Ph.D. from University of Michigan and is an Associate Professor at the University of Texas at Arlington. Her research and teaching focus on literary theory, semiotics, hermeneutics, eighteenth and twentieth-century German thought, theory of myth, psychoanalysis, pre-Hindu Indian deity Lajja gauri, and Mexican painter Olga Dondé. She has published on Heidegger, Hamann/Herder, Kleist, Rilke, and Foucault. Professor Frank organized and chaired a national conference on "Literature and the Occult" and an international conference on "The Female Principle." She edited two collections of scholarly essays and co-translated and introduced Emil Staiger's construction of a Heideggerian genre theory, *Grundbegriffe der Poetik* [Basic Concepts of Poetics], to English readers.

PIETER LEMMENS teaches philosophy and ethics at Radboud University in Nijmegen, the Netherlands. He has published on themes in the philosophy of technology and innovation (open source and commons-based), on the work of Martin Heidegger, Peter Sloterdijk and Bernard Stiegler, on the Anthropocene as well as on post-operaist Marxism (Hardt, Negri, Berardi) and on themes from philosophical anthropology and postphenomenology. He translated Stiegler's *Philosopher par accident* to Dutch (2014) and co-edited a book on the philosophy of landscape and place (2011) as well as a volume on contemporary German philosophy (2013), both in Dutch. He is currently preparing a monograph on the work of Stiegler and an introductory book to the philosophy of technology. Current interests are the philosophical and politico-economic aspects of human (cognitive) enhancement technologies, the philosophy of psychedelics and philosophy of technology in the age of the Anthropocene.

TRACY POWELL holds a Ph.D. in Educational Psychology from Simon Fraser University in British Columbia, Canada. She teaches in the Psychology Department, Behavioral Sciences Division at Western Oregon University. Her research interests focus on philosophical applications of psychology in law, particularly as it relates to the understandings of self, narrative truth, and consciousness.

MARTA GRACIELA TRÓGOLO is a full professor in modern philosophy both in the College of Humanities and in the College of Economic Sciences at Universidad Nacional del Nordeste, Argentina. She has been a permanent researcher at UNNE since 1999 and contributes to a collaborative working group on Agency of the Body: Facticity, and Symbolic Representation for Social Inclusion.

MARC VAN DEN BOSSCHE is a full-time professor in the Department of Philosophy and Moral Sciences at the Vrije Universiteit Brussel (VUB). He is the author of *Kritiek van de Technische Rede* [*Critique of Technical Reason*] (Leuven/Utrecht 1995), *Natuur en Lijfelijkheid* [Nature and Embodiment/Physicality] (Utrecht 1998), and *Ironie en Solidariteit. Een Kennismaking met het Werk van Richard Rorty* [*Irony and Solidarity: An Introduction to the Work of Richard Rorty*] (Rotterdam 2001), *Het Pathos van het Denken* [*The Pathos of Thinking*], *Religie na de Dood van God* [Religion after the Death of God], *De Zinnen van het Leven. Of de Kunst van het Verstaan* [*The Meanings of Life. Or the Art of Understanding*] and *Vreemde Wereld. Zygmunt Bauman over Samenleven in Vloeibare Tijden* [*Strange World: Zygmunt Bauman on Living in Liquid Times*]. Van den Bossche also wrote essays on subjectivity and intersubjectivity as well as two bestsellers: *Wielrennen* [*Cycling*] and *Sport als Levenskunst* [*Sports as an Art of Living*] (Rotterdam 2005 and 2010). He is the editor and co-editor of book volumes on Rorty, Arendt, Fukuyama and several topics in the history of philosophy. His current research focuses on migration, art, and social imaginaries.

GALIT WELLNER, Ph.D., is a senior lecturer at the NB School of Design in Haifa, Israel. She is also an adjunct professor at Tel Aviv University. Galit studies digital technologies and their inter-relations with humans. She is active in the postphenomenology community that studies philosophy of technology. She published several peer-reviewed articles and book chapters. Her book *A Postphenomenological Inquiry of Cellphones: Genealogies, Meanings and Becoming* was published in 2015 by Lexington Books. She translated to Hebrew Don Ihde's *Postphenomenology and Technoscience* (Resling 2016). She also co-edited *Postphenomenology and Media: Essays on Human–Media–World Relations* (Lexington Books 2017).

PROCEEDINGS

SOCIETY FOR PHENOMENOLOGY AND MEDIA

www.ingramcontent.com/pod-product-compliance
Lightning Source LLC
Chambersburg PA
CBHW081017040426
42444CB00014B/3240